TWENTIETH CENTURY INTERPRETATIONS

OF

THE NIGGER

OF THE

"NARCISSUS"

A Collection of Critical Essays

Edited by
JOHN A. PALMER

Prentice-Hall, Inc. *Englewood Cliffs, N. J.*

A SPECTRUM BOOK

Quotations from *The Nigger of the "Narcissus"* by Joseph
Conrad used by permission of J. M. Dent & Sons, Ltd.

Current printing (last number):
10 9 8 7 6 5 4 3 2 1

PRENTICE-HALL INTERNATIONAL, INC. (*London*)
PRENTICE-HALL OF AUSTRALIA, PTY. LTD. (*Sydney*)
PRENTICE-HALL OF CANADA, LTD. (*Toronto*)
PRENTICE-HALL OF INDIA PRIVATE LIMITED (*New Delhi*)
PRENTICE-HALL OF JAPAN, INC. (*Tokyo*)

Contents

Introduction

by John A. Palmer

I

On April 28, 1884, the Polish-English seaman Józef Teodor Konrad Nałęcz Korzeniowski left Bombay aboard the sailing vessel *Narcissus,* a ship he had singled out, according to his own account, solely for her loveliness and grace. Six months later, having survived a fierce gale south of the Cape of Good Hope, the ship docked at Dunkirk. And some thirteen years after that, the novelist Joseph Conrad transmuted this experience into a work of fictional art that his contemporary Henry James hailed as the "finest and strongest picture of the sea and sea-life that our language possesses."

Conrad's maritime career was a distinguished one, marred only by his temperamental restlessness and by the gradual encroachment of steam and steel on the microcosm of the sailing vessel in which he had found his first identity. His voyages took him far from Poland and England, to the islands of the Far East and even into the savage Africa he had read about as a boy. Conrad became a Master mariner in the British merchant service before reaching thirty—a striking achievement for a man who had left his homeland only twelve years before, with no seagoing experience and little knowledge of English. But his literary career was even more remarkable. Spanning some three decades (until his death in 1924), during which time he produced half a dozen works which are likely to remain classics of English fiction and twenty or thirty others which will continue to excite his admirers, it made Conrad one of the most famous and respected of modern novelists, with an influence extending to such diverse writers as James, Mann, Gide, Fitzgerald, Faulkner, Eliot, and the French existentialists.

Conrad was almost forty when *The Nigger of the "Narcissus"* began to run in *The New Review,* and had first appeared in print only two years before, with *Almayer's Folly.* But his literary interests and motives had developed early. Apollo Korzeniowski, Conrad's father, had been a poet and translator—as well as revolutionary—and the young Conrad had grown up an avid reader of books. Among his favorites were volumes of travel and adventure: Cooper, Marryat, Hugo's *Travailleurs de la Mer,* and records of exploration like those of Park and Livingstone. Conrad's boyhood reading, his loneliness after the family's exile from Poland in 1862, and then the early deaths of his parents, instilled in him a sense of isolation and a love of the exotic he never quite lost. These bitter early experiences also left their mark, however, in hidden emotional conflicts that sometimes reached the level of psychosis. Conrad's attempted suicide as a youth in Marseilles, his persistent depression and hypochondria, and his irascibility toward family and friends during his long grey years in the English country- side were visible marks of the fears and guilts that found less direct expression in much of his fiction. Although *The Nigger of the "Nar- cissus"* is freer of these conflicts than most of Conrad's other major works, the reader must be prepared nonetheless for the dark side of Conrad. The *Nigger* is a lyric tribute to lost companions and the lost world of the sailing vessel; it is an affirmation of human solidarity and of the "few very simple ideas" Conrad offered as the ethical core of his work. But it is also an ambivalent work, with strains of feeling that some early reviewers thought "grim" and "brutal," and a deep- lying background of metaphysical skepticism that was always inter- fused, however unconsciously, with Conrad's private conflicts. The reader must approach the *Nigger* cautiously, with an expectation of multiple, perhaps even contradictory, meanings, and with a willing- ness to apply sophisticated criteria of literary judgment.

The *Nigger* was not an immediate commercial success (Conrad was not to write a best seller until *Chance,* in 1912). Its early readers were aware of the novel's descriptive power and the authenticity of its account of shipboard life; and reviewers compared Conrad favorably with such nineteenth-century exotic novelists as Stevenson, Kipling, Cooper, Loti, and Melville. Conrad's literary contemporaries—men like James and Bennett and Cunninghame Graham—were even more enthusiastic (a "crackerjack," Stephen Crane called the book). Yet many readers recognized also that Conrad's uncompromising artistic integrity might limit his audience, and others confessed themselves unable to see any significant idea beneath the splendid surface of Conrad's tale. Despite their hesitant acknowledgement of Conrad's genius, these early critics were simply misled by their own literary experience. Devoid of the usual trappings of the adventure tale, lack- ing the conventional heroine and even a conventional hero, peopled with life-sized human beings instead of out-sized romantic types, the *Nigger* bears only the most tenuous relationships to the kind of fiction with which it was at first compared.

The Nigger of the "Narcissus" is one of those freaks of literature, a great original work; and its true dimensions have been revealed only during the last few decades, as the instruments of modern critical analysis have been sharpened and refined. The essays reprinted here form a dialectic in which all the important issues relating to the *Nigger* are debated, as well as many important issues relating to Conrad's work and to modern fiction as a whole. The *Nigger* has in fact become a paradigm case for the testing of assumptions about point of view, symbolism, structure, and style in fiction; and the reader of this volume will find himself drawn into some sharp critical controversies.

II

Conrad has often been called a romantic; and this label is useful, especially if certain superficially "romantic" aspects of his work, like the persistent exoticism and baroque style of his early fiction, are set aside. In common with many nineteenth-century writers, Conrad tended to view commerce and machinery and material progress—"the land," wherever he is employing the symbolic dichotomy of land-and-sea—as destructive of human sensibility and self-reliance (this is one source of his hostility toward steam-driven vessels); insofar as the men of the *Narcissus* achieve self-discovery and self-purgation through direct interaction with the forces of nature, they fulfill a characteristic romantic aim. And several writers have noted the Wordsworthian socioesthetic ideal of the *Nigger's* famous Preface, with its appeal to something "more permanently enduring" than wisdom: "the latent feeling of fellowship with all creation—and to the subtle but invincible conviction of solidarity . . . which binds men to each other, which binds together all humanity—the dead to the living and the living to the unborn" (p. viii).[1]

But Conrad's romanticism was never Rousseauist or theological. Like most late-Victorian attitudes, it was conditioned by the relentless discoveries of evolutionary science and an increasing sense of alienation from a mechanistic universe. Cecil Scrimgeour, Ian Watt, and

---

[1] Unless otherwise indicated, page references throughout this volume are to the Dent Collected Edition of Conrad's works. Most other Dent and Doubleday editions have identical pagination.

other writers have called attention to a letter written just after Conrad had finished the *Nigger,* in which he imagines nature as a vast knitting machine which has "evolved itself . . . out of a chaos of scraps of iron," and "goes on knitting" despite the observer's protest: "the infamous thing has made itself: made itself without thought, without conscience, without foresight, without eyes, without heart. . . . It knits us in and it knits us out. It has knitted time, space, death, corruption, despair, and all the illusions—and nothing matters." The sense of helplessness and meaninglessness, the conviction that man has lost his gods and stands alone in the face of an overwhelmingly powerful and indifferent universe, haunts all of Conrad's fiction, from the storm scenes of the *Nigger,* to the *Patna* episode of *Lord Jim,* to Decoud's final moments in *Nostromo,* to the metaphysical allegory of *Victory*; and it lends depth and poignancy to the apparently casual phrases Conrad uses to describe the world of the *Narcissus's* crew: "a great circular solitude" (p. 29), "the vast silence of pain and labour" (p. 90). Like Crane's characters in "The Open Boat," who find the Star of Bethlehem reduced to "a high cold star on a winter's night," the *Narcissus* seems "to beckon in vain for help towards the stormy sky" (p. 49); and her crew must confront an inversion of traditional Christian values, with "grace" and "mercy" now vested ironically in the indifferent sea (p. 90). And as Ian Watt has observed, Conrad was doubly alienated, since he could not even accept the idea of a secular paradise propagated by the nineteenth-century disciples of "progress."

In a valuable recent study, J. Hillis Miller finds Conrad finally the premier exponent of nihilism in English fiction: "From Dickens and George Eliot through Trollope, Meredith, and Hardy the negative implications of subjectivism become more and more apparent. It remained for Conrad to explore nihilism to its depths, and, in doing so, to point the way toward the transcendence of nihilism by the poets of the twentieth century" (*Poets of Reality,* p. 6). Setting aside for the moment the question whether, and to what extent, Conrad himself succeeded in transcending his own nihilism, Miller's formulation gives some idea of the strength of Conrad's metaphysical despair and of the importance of the symbolism of darkness and chaos in his fiction. Conrad's deepest premises suggest that the insight of the Preface's ideal artist (or that of old Singleton as he comprehends fully the fact of his own mortality) will reveal ultimately only a dark negation beneath the arbitrary forms and rituals of human life. Man's ideas and ideals are his own creation; he remains cut off from the truth of the universe, in an illusion-filled and dreamlike state, except during those moments of supreme vision when he does encounter the "darkness"—source and terminus of all life, and the denial of all sensory qualities and human concepts. Confronted with death and the sea's measureless destructive power—forces which disrupt shipboard ritual and test solidarity to its breaking point—the men of the *Narcissus* discover that the problem of life is "too voluminous for the narrow limits of human speech" (p. 138). Characters like Kurtz and Lord Jim and Decoud and Heyst, in later works of Conrad, make the same discovery even more profoundly and face its destructive implications even more directly. In *The Nigger of the "Narcissus"* Conrad was still working his way toward a coherent metaphysical attitude. But the voyage of the *Narcissus* is projected against a backdrop which holds latent within itself all the despair of Conrad's most pessimistic visions.

III

If Captain Allistoun and old Singleton seem somehow to rise above the sentimentality and fear of the rest of the crew, and to stand firm against the dual threat to the *Narcissus,* their understanding remains almost wordless, revealing itself largely through force of will and grim fidelity to duty. In contrast, the loquacious labor agitator Donkin attempts to manipulate his mates and disrupt their loyalty to the ship. As James E. Miller, Jr. observes in his pioneering study of the *Nigger,* the novel's basic dramatic structure is generated from this conflict: "Donkin and Singleton . . . represent opposed attitudes toward death and life (symbolized respectively by Wait and the sea), attitudes which vie with each other to dominate the crew." In winning through to the "primitive wisdom" of Singleton, which accepts life and death for what they are, and sustaining finally the "solidarity . . . which binds men to each other and all mankind to the visible world" (p. xiv), the crew brings Conrad's novel to an essentially optimistic conclusion, despite the threats posed by a dark and enigmatic universe. But this optimistic conclusion obviously raises the question of the novel's present relevance. Was not Conrad merely attempting to reclaim a hopelessly outmoded tradition, one based on values too simple and too conservative to withstand the complexities of modern life? And even supposing "solidarity" could be defined in some still viable way, would it not then be swept away into Conrad's "darkness" by the kind of nihilistic argument suggested above? Marvin Mudrick would answer "yes" to the first question, and J. Hillis Miller "yes" to the second; and their case is formidable. Yet Ian Watt argues per-

suasively, in his brilliant essay in *The English Mind,* that Conrad's
ethical position may be seen as a legitimate, if tenuous, counterbalance to the alienation of the modern mind. "Solidarity," Watt
says, may be defined as

> an intangible and undemonstrable but existent and widespread accept-
> ance of common human obligations which somehow transcend the infi-
> nite individual differences of belief and purpose and taste. It is not a
> conscious motive, and it rarely becomes the dominating factor in human
> affairs; its existence seems to depend very largely upon the mere fact that,
> in the course of their different lives, most individuals find themselves
> faced with very similar circumstances; nevertheless, it is solidarity which
> gives both the individual and the collective life what little pattern of
> meaning can be discovered in it. Conrad's own experience, of course,
> tended to confirm this view of solidarity; and his most typical writing
> is concerned to present its achievements, to enact its discovery, or to assay
> its powers (pp. 270–71).

Insofar as this limited form of commitment takes the condition of
the alienated individual as its starting point, and rejects the notion
of *a priori* values, it bears affinities with modern existentialism; insofar
as it requires corporate social activity to generate itself, it bears
affinities with modern collectivist theories; and insofar as it involves
a reaffirmation of common human obligations, including the restraints
of honor and duty, it bears affinities with modern ethical conservatism.
When coupled with Conrad's conscious effort to make the broadest
possible ethical appeal in his work (an aim announced both in the
Preface and in his 1895 Author's Note to *Almayer's Folly*), these theoretical affinities, as Watt remarks, may help to account for the continuing interest in Conrad as a moralist. If a sense of solidarity is
generated merely by the conditions of human existence, then it will
by definition escape the nihilism that destroys the certainty of everything but that existence. And if the writer of fiction can really "present its achievements," "enact its discovery," and "assay its powers,"
then he can, through the medium of his art, help modern man fight
his sense of alienation. Ultimately these are matters each reader must
grapple with himself—perhaps in the first instance by confronting
several of Conrad's major works—but the issues are significant and
the final answers meaningful.

　　The depth and realism of Conrad's "few very simple ideas" are
indicated in his attitude toward the more sentimental and charitable
aspects of the Christian ethic. As Vernon Young observes, the crew of
the *Narcissus* commit the sin of pride and endanger the ship even
further by encouraging Wait's malignity; for Conrad, "to return good

for evil is not only profoundly immoral but dangerous, in that it sharpens the appetite for evil in the malevolent and develops (perhaps unconsciously) that latent tendency towards hyprocrisy in the . . . let us say, benevolent" (from a letter quoted by Young). Judgments like these, based on Conrad's awareness of the persistent darkness in all men, are the ethical counterparts of his grimly realistic metaphysics. And Wait's and Donkin's transgressions can be measured only in terms of these fundamental ethical ideas. Watt asserts that Wait has done no "evil," but given Conrad's notion of solidarity, "evil" is probably not too bold a term. Wait's derelictions—malingering, evasion of duty, manipulation of others, unmanly fear—are precise inversions of the fidelity and commitment to human community, and above all of the courage to face a final darkness, that are essential ingredients of Conrad's ethics. On the everyday level, these inversions may merely create grotesque comedy: Jimmy stealthily refusing his medicine or revelling in Donkin's abuse (a form of comedy, by the way, that prefigures the more persistent grotesqueries of the metaphysically inverted Jones gang in *Victory*). But at climactic moments in the action—during Jimmy's final agonies, or on the threshold of the crew's mutiny—they wear a more serious cast.

The most obvious value-inverter aboard the *Narcissus* is of course Donkin, the "man that cannot steer" (p. 10). In leading the cry to cut masts when the *Narcissus* is on her side, he would abandon all chance to restore the order of the ship; and nowhere is his opposition to the resolute helmsman Singleton more clearly marked. As Avrom Fleishman and Norris W. Yates demonstrate, Donkin is Conrad's chief vehicle in *The Nigger of the "Narcissus"* for expressing his skepticism toward theories of socioeconomic reform (just as the cook, with his "supreme conceit" (p. 116) and loss of humanity, is Conrad's chief vehicle for satirizing any species of reform based on supernatural assurances). Donkin's mutinous behavior and soapbox oratory proceed from a combination of incompetence, laziness, and personal greed; at the crucial dramatic moment with Captain Allistoun forcing the belaying pin back upon him, both his argument and his courage fail; and Conrad scornfully sends him back to the land: "Donkin, who never did a decent day's work in his life, no doubt earns his living by discoursing with filthy eloquence upon the right of labour to live. So be it! Let the earth and the sea each have its own" (p. 172). Conrad's ethical democracy was not a social democracy. He recognized a natural aristocracy, founded in part on age and experience; and he scoffed at the notion of "a wealthy and well-fed crew of satisfied skippers" (p. 103). But his principal objections to the kind of social idealism represented by the reformers of his day went deeper than any mere social conservatism or authoritarianism. Conrad's political skepticism was rooted in ethical and metaphysical beliefs about the individual's responsibility to save himself and the extraordinary difficulty, perhaps the impossibility, of doing so; he was deeply suspicious of the self-announced altruism and rationality of political idealists; and he saw political idealism and economic instrumentalism as essentially divisive, setting one group or individual against another, in violation of their greater ties to the human community. These ideas were to emerge more fully and more sharply in such works as *The Secret Agent* and *Under Western Eyes,* but most of them are implicit in Conrad's treatment of Donkin.

In the end, of course, Donkin is defeated; and the crew is able to preserve its solidarity even in the face of the land's distractions:

> Outside, on Tower Hill, they blinked, hesitated clumsily, as if blinded by the strange quality of the hazy light, as if discomposed by the view of so many men; and they who could hear one another in the howl of gales seemed deafened and distracted by the full roar of the busy earth—"To the Black Horse! To the Black Horse!" cried some. "Let us have a drink together before we part." They crossed the road, clinging to one another (p. 170).

But there are obvious elements of ambiguity in Conrad's final attitudes in the *Nigger:* despite the profusion of light as the *Narcissus* triumphantly enters her berth, the crew is seen finally as a "dark knot of seamen"; Charley, the youngest crewman, and Belfast, the persistent sentimentalist, fail to achieve even the uncertain camaraderie of the others, wandering off alone; and the officers and narrator disdain the visible symbolism of the Black Horse and the shared drink, which corrupts the spiritual quality of the crew's solidarity and involves it in the artifice and delusion of the land. If the narrator can see the crew finally as "a good crowd" who have "wrung out a meaning" from their "sinful lives," he never loses sight of their littleness and their impotence. And this persistent ethical ambivalence involves Conrad in some difficult technical problems. As Guerard has observed, Conrad was forced to discover a means of modulating upward from the everyday level of the crew's shipboard existence to the spiritual heroics of the storm scenes, then back downward toward the crew's antiheroic involvement with Donkin's mutiny and with James Wait in his final throes, then upward again to the symbolic climax of Jimmy's burial at sea—moving, as it were, from pole to pole of the author's own sense of the human dilemma. Only by removing the narrative focus from the crew, and placing it on the ship itself as it approaches the land and enters its berth, was he able to sustain the exalted tone of the final pages without sacrificing the complexity of his own feelings. In these, as in other ways, *The Nigger of the "Narcissus"* is a triumph of the fiction writer's art; and the sensitive reader will wish to turn finally to certain technical aspects of the novel which help to display Conrad's artistry at its best, but which have aroused some critical controversy of the highest order.

IV

Guerard's observations about the final narrative perspective of the *Nigger,* in which the ship itself seems to supplant the crew as protagonist, are closely related to a familiar critical problem with this novel—what Guerard calls the "waywardness" of its point of view, as the narrative voice shifts from "they" to "we" and finally to "I," oscillating between the limited vision of a crew member and the unrestricted vision of an "omniscient" narrator. Young, Guerard, Mudrick, and Watt, among the writers represented in this volume, consider the issue in some detail. Everyone seems to agree with Guerard that such shifts are harmless so long as they do not "violate the reader's larger sustained vision of the dramatized experience"—but there is considerable difference as to what precisely that vision is, so that specific variations remain controversial. Guerard argues persuasively that the point of view varies in such a way as to reflect the novel's "general movement from isolation to solidarity to poignant separation" (and is thus organic, it may be noted, to the dramatic movement set forth in James Miller's essay). Guerard objects only to the narrator's having access to Wait's interior monologues, since "it has been the very convention of the novel that Wait must remain shadowy, vast, provocative of large speculation: in a word, symbolic." We may observe that Jimmy's monologues (like the final scenes between Wait and Donkin, which similarly are inaccessible except to an "omniscient" narrator) help to develop the antiromantic strains of Conrad's tale: Jimmy's fear of his impending death is the romantic egoist's fear of self-dissolution, and his nightmare visions prefigure the nihilistic "horror" of Kurtz's final moments in "Heart of Darkness." But these narrative shifts into the omniscient mode (as distinguished from the mere grammatical third person) interfere with the symbolic functions of Wait and Donkin, as the crew progresses toward Singleton's primitive wisdom and the reaffirmation of solidarity implicit in it. Insofar as the focal point of the reader's experience lies with the novel's protagonists—insofar as it is Conrad's aim, in other words, to draw the reader through the crew's experience toward a vicarious affirmation of solidarity—sudden glimpses into the privacy of Wait's cabin and into the privacy of his mind do seem illicit, perhaps even raising Mudrick's question of "the artist's conscience."

Ian Watt, with the chance to say the last word on the subject (at least among the critics in this volume) provides a comprehensive discussion of point of view in the *Nigger*; but his excellent summary hardly closes the issue. It is probable, for example, that the relations between Conrad's pronoun usage and his multiple artistic purposes in the *Nigger* have been insufficiently explored: "they" whenever he is thinking of his old shipmates as a departed generation and so is conscious of his separation from them in time, or when he is separated rhetorically from them and functioning as chorus or judge; "we" when he is recalling the action of the novel, particularly (and with appropriate humility) during the crew's more regressive moments; "I" when the narrative has reached its climax and he wishes to move from the dramatic structure into a final lyric tribute. Moreover, the whole question of point of view in fiction is bound up intimately with broader theories about the purpose of literature, assumptions barely visible in the specific dispute, say, between Mudrick and Watt. Without pretending to explicate these assumptions fully, it may be possible to identify at least one important view of literature that does have considerable bearing on recent technical discussions of Conrad's art—namely, the theory that literature is an instrument of knowledge, with its own unique epistemological conventions. This view has been developed in its most sophisticated forms by philosopher-critics who have studied the general question of symbolism (Ernst Cassirer, Susanne Langer, and others) and by theorists of the "New Criticism" of the 1930's and 1940's (such writers as Cleanth Brooks, John Crowe Ransom, and Mark Schorer). Underlying most of their discussions is the paradigm figure of Man (and hence author and reader) as an existential being cut off from supernatural sources of knowledge and faced with choices between alternative symbolic records of experience —history, science, myth, poetry—each with its own validity and its own rules of discourse. Poetry and myth, rooted in immediate perception and committed to forms and to a species of language which tend to hold opposites in suspension, cannot produce the empirical generalizations of science or the reasoned conclusions of philosophy, but yield instead a heightened sense of human dilemmas, and of Man's ultimately paradoxical relation to his universe. At the risk of over-simplification, something like this seems to lie behind Mudrick's objections to Conrad's "violation" of point of view in the *Nigger*. The represented experience—the dilemma faced by the crew as they try to cope with the claims of Wait and Donkin, and their growth toward Singleton's sense of more profound paradoxes, both metaphysical and ethical—can be dramatized only from the point of view of a crewman, so that Conrad's flights into omniscience, or into the nostalgic coda of the final paragraphs, may seem unconscionable elements of impurity in the literary performance: a presumption of superior knowledge and a jumping ahead, as it were, to conclusions which may or may not emerge from the dramatized experience. A critic less committed to a particular paradigm of literature-as-knowledge, one who, like Watt, does not mind even "a veritable Pooh-Bah of perscrutation" as narrator, will not find these abrupt shifts so troublesome, provided they serve a legitimate rhetorical function.

Mudrick's resistance to Conrad's conservative ethical assumptions, particularly when they are expressed abstractly, may be traceable in part to the same general view of literature. If one of the distinguishing marks of poetry (and fiction) as a unique kind of discourse is its involvement in immediate perception—in the primary ground, one may say, of Man's relation to his universe—then concreteness is a *sine qua non,* and the author must restrict himself to such abstractions as may grow out of the perceptual experience. "My task," Conrad says in his Preface, "which I am trying to achieve is, by the power of the written word to make you hear, to make you feel—it is, before all, to make you *see.* That—and no more, and it is everything" (p. x). Much of the *Nigger* does have the virtue of a hard perceptual realism, despite some impressionistic blurring and late-Victorian literary inhibition; but much of it, too, like the famous first paragraph of Chapter Four, may strike the reader as unnecessarily remote. Guerard's remarks about Conrad's "art of modulation" and Ian Watt's analogy between Conrad's purple passages and the Greek chorus provide considerable rhetorical justification for the variations in Conrad's style; but crucial issues are at stake here; and Mudrick's article serves to remind us of the danger, for the novelist, in departing from the unique norms of fictional discourse—experience highly imaged, and rendered in sufficient detail to capture its subtlest implications and contradictions.

V

By far the most controversial aspect of the *Nigger*, however, has been its alleged "symbolic" or "mythic" quality. As Zabel has observed, Conrad "is doing what all tellers of the tales of ships have done, from Homer in the *Odyssey* or the satirists of the *Narrenschiff* and *Ship of Fools* to Cooper, Dana, and Melville. He is making of the *Narcissus* and her crew a world, an image of humanity on its hazardous voyage into the elements, the future, the unknown" (*Craft and Character*, p. 180). From the beginning, the reader sees this universalizing thrust: in the carefully mixed nationalities of the crew, in the figure of the ship as "a small planet" surrounded by "the abysses of sky and sea" (p. 29), in portentous symbolic invocations like Wait's " 'I belong to the ship' " (p. 18), and the like. But its exact nature and extent—and more important, its justification—are questions still unresolved, despite the extended commentary of critics like Guerard and Watt. Half ironically, Watt invents four new terms to specify the possible ways in which the meanings of Conrad's narrative might be enlarged: *homeophor,* which works "by natural extension of the implications of the narrative content, and retains a consistent closeness to it"; *heterophor,* which "carries us to *another* meaning . . . *beyond* any demonstrable connection between the literary object and the symbolic meaning given it"; *mythophor,* which relates the literary object to another story, i.e., to "a specific body of mythical, religious, or literary knowledge"; and *cryptophor,* which relates the object to an unconscious analogue or "story" like those associated with the names of Freud and Jung. A brief discussion of the *Nigger* need not attempt to examine each dimension in turn (a task in any case best left to the critics in this volume); but the variety of possibilities suggested by Watt's terms may make the reader wary of too "realistic" a reading.

There are, to begin with, some fairly obvious ways Conrad manipulates his plot and imagery to create symbolic suggestions. As Vernon Young and others have pointed out, the physical weather met by the *Narcissus* and the inner moral weather of her crew parallel one another closely, from the dreamlike haze of the voyage's first days, to the chaos and formlessness of the gale, to the enforced Coleridgean calm as Jimmy awaits death ("The universe conspired with James Wait"—p. 143), to the breeze that springs up obediently after his burial, to the triumphant bright sunshine of the ship's final berthing—a continuing artifice which makes clear that the elements threatening the *Narcissus* lie within its crew as well as without, and helps to justify a mythophoric reading like Scrimgeour's: Conrad's nihilistic version, as it were, of the ancient epic convention of a moral alliance between protagonist and cosmic forces. Perhaps equally obvious are the symbolic oppositions of light-and-darkness and land-and-sea, motifs discussed effectively by Young and others. Insofar as these manipulations of plot and image serve merely to extend the ethical and metaphysical meanings implicit in the novel's more basic elements—in action, character, and thought as identified by James Miller, for example— they serve the comparatively modest purposes of Watt's "homeophor," and arouse little disagreement.

When a symbolic reading extends to specific characters, however, or begins to seem too restrictive, the critic will encounter more resistance. For reasons suggested in the last section, allegory—which tends to dramatize conclusions rather than explore dilemmas, and to limit characters to single meanings—has become a less viable mode for the modern fictionist, so that the critic who unnecessarily "allegorizes" a character seems to do his author a disservice. (Watt perhaps unfairly brings this charge against James Miller, since Miller acknowledges the existence of secondary structures outside the scope of his essay, and uses "symbol" merely to identify certain characters as focal points of values Conrad was interested in, without limiting their significance to those values. But Watt's remarks do suggest some of the dangers inherent in any symbolic reading.) The sharpest case in point, of course, is James Wait. Although Watt and Guerard, among others, analyze Wait's symbolic functions in some detail, it is worth adding a few remarks here to help relate Wait to the themes and symbolic motifs discussed elsewhere in this Introduction, and to bring into focus the inevitable modern question of Conrad's racial attitudes.

Something has already been said of Wait's place in the ethical and dramatic structure of the *Nigger:* as a reminder of impending death, he provides a focal point for the opposed attitudes of Singleton and Donkin; and in his own malingering, self-pity, and fear, he provides a kind of antiethical paradigm for the crew. "He was demoralising," the narrator says: "through him we were becoming highly humanised, tender, complex, excessively decadent: we understood the subtlety of his fear, sympathised with all his repulsions, shrinkings, evasions, delusions—as though we had been overcivilised, and rotten, and without any knowledge of the meaning of life" (p. 139). But to fall victim to these "repulsions, shrinkings, evasions, delusions" is also to descend toward "darkness," toward the merely instinctive and precivilized, so that Wait can be seen also as "animal-like . . . a scared brute" (p. 118), or "a black buoy chained to the bottom of a muddy stream" (p. 138). And Conrad's use of a black man to symbolize these motifs of ethical and evolutionary regression has several causes. There is, first of all, the archetypal association of darkness with ignorance; to extend this association to men with black skins is of course fallacious, but the social climate of Conrad's time made it easy for him to indulge the fallacy. Moreover, Wait's uncomplicated fears, his simple deceptions (even self-deceptions), childish aggressions, and resentments do seem to have been characteristic of the primitive peoples Conrad visited—at least as Conrad remembered them. If Conrad's experience was incomplete, and if historical events have made us more painfully aware of the dangers of anthropological synecdoche, the fault need not be laid too heavily on Conrad. Finally, we must remember that "darkness" is always heterophoric for Conrad: like any prolific and complex writer, he tended to develop a private symbolic language (poets like Blake and Yeats and Stevens are more obvious examples, but the principle holds for many novelists as well); and in this context, Wait gathers symbolic overtones the reader might otherwise have missed. The same applies to Donkin, who is described in animal imagery so often as to suggest a close relationship to such later Conrad characters as Verloc and the Jones gang, and who is related to Wait through metaphors associated more directly with Jimmy himself (e.g., Donkin first appears as if "wandering in sunshine: a startling visitor from a world of nightmares" (p. 10). In a variety of ways, Conrad's story and characters invite complex readings of the kind provided by Guerard and Scrimgeour and Young; and the reader who would see the novel as a whole must be continuously alert to such symbolic suggestions.

At the same time, rational limits to literary "interpretation" do exist, and it will be useful to identify some of these before exposure to the multiple persuasions of the critics in this volume. To begin with, the reader obviously must ask himself whether the text really establishes and sustains the suggested meanings, and whether they are consistent with meanings established by greater masses of detail and by more fundamental elements of the novel, like the Aristotelian plot structure described by James Miller. Vernon Young's notion that "West" is equated with "death" in the *Nigger,* for example, probably ought to be viewed skeptically, since some details (e.g., Jimmy's being a West Indian black) support it, and some (e.g., the final homeward movement of the *Narcissus*) do not. Similarly, the motifs of the

Odyssey and the Dance of Death are probably less important than Scrimgeour's opening remarks suggest. Conrad's prepolitical ethical focus, his isolated and microcosmic setting, and his symbolic drama of man against the elements do make the *Nigger* at its deepest levels analogous to myth; and the parallels Scrimgeour finds are certainly present. But they are not sufficiently developed to invite extended attention; and they lie largely dormant even in Scrimgeour's own essay, serving to energize a series of excellent insights into the novel, especially its metaphysical dimensions, without helping much to crystallize the reader's final perception of the novel's symbolic structures. The critic's task is to discover how such symbolic overtones may extend the significance of the represented action, without permitting them to preempt the critical discussion or to obscure more directly visible meanings.

A more specific problem is related to the novel's shifting point of view, discussed earlier. Some of the invitations to a symbolic reading of the *Nigger* are offered only in the first person plural—the voice of the involved participant in the crew's experience—and this of course raises the question of their validity. If it is only in the eyes of the incompletely initiated seamen that Wait seems a "black idol" (p. 105) or that "a black mist" (p. 34) seems to emanate from him, thus building a metaphorical bridge between Wait and the universe of dark water that threatens the *Narcissus,* the reader may not be persuaded to accept the parallel ethical responses that such metaphors would justify. But it is in fact the "outer," third person narrator who initiates and sustains the mode of symbolic suggestion—in the opening pages, with their play of darkness-and-light, in the abstract philosophical passages near the middle, and in the final passages of rhetorical conclusion. Moreover, the boldness with which this highest narrative voice exercises its metaphorical prerogative increases as the novel progresses, passing from mere configurations of imagery, through abstract asides, to a final fusion of these two modes in the famous docking and pay-room passages. In sum, the total narrative context seems to invite us to view the men's tentative symbolic renditions of their experience, like their moral responses generally, as more-or-less successful essays toward a final state of metaphysical and ethical understanding represented fully only by the outside narrator himself; and with this qualification, their metaphorical experiments can probably be integrated safely into a reading of the novel.

Finally, it is important to ask precisely what is being affirmed in any given symbolic interpretation: whether, for example, the "interpretation" is really an analysis of meanings, or bears some other relationship to the text. For illustration, we may compare Guerard's interpretation of Wait's rescue as a symbolic rebirth with Young's more Jungian view of the rescue as effecting "a respite, a temporary release from danger, in the manner of the old tales in which an ogre was freed from a cave, a witch from an oak-tree or an imp from a bottle." Guerard's reading, which rests upon explicit references to the birth analogue (Wait's head thrust at a tiny hole, for example, or his "blooming short wool"—p. 70) helps to extend the motifs of regression and infantilism associated with Wait, and imposes a monumental irony on the death theme: in assisting at Wait's rescue, the men symbolically affirm a continuity of life even in the face of Wait's decline, just as they do in coping successfully with the outer threat to the *Narcissus*. Young's view, on the other hand, is essentially extraliterary. The reader's unconscious response to archetypal narrative patterns of the kind identified by Young may help account for an unanalyzable emotional potential in the rescue scene, beyond that justified by the details of the conscious literary experience. But the ultimate effect of such an analysis may be to lessen the story's power by explaining away emotional irrelevancies based on these unconscious analogues—a process which purifies the reader's response without adding anything to it. (A well-known example is the psychiatrist Ernest Jones's discussion of *Hamlet* in terms of Hamlet's, and ultimately Shakespeare's, Oedipus complex. Some of his friends—playgoers who had apparently substituted the pleasures of unconscious titillation for the more genuine dramatic pleasures resting in the thematic complexity and structural coherence of Shakespeare's work—complained that Jones's analysis had diminished the play for them.) In contrast, Guerard's reading builds upon meanings already established in the text and remains consistent with its other narrative elements. Neither Guerard nor Young draws the distinction clearly, but it is perhaps fair to say that Guerard's reading of the rescue scene is a symbolic interpretation, while Young's reading is really a causal explanation of some of its extraliterary power. By keeping such distinctions in mind, and by refusing to accept any reading which would violate the pattern of meanings established by more obvious and more powerful rhetorical and symbolic structures, the reader can admit the full richness of Conrad's novel and at the same time guard himself against the excesses of Conrad's admirers.

VI

The Nigger of the "Narcissus" is not Conrad's best work. This honor must fall finally on such later novels as "Heart of Darkness" and *Lord Jim* and *The Secret Agent.* But it is in many ways his most characteristic, fusing as it does his intimate knowledge of the sea and his deepest ethical convictions. The lingering romanticism of the *Nigger*—the assumption, for example, that men *will* finally, under sufficient pressure, sustain the solidarity that is so important to Conrad —will be further eroded as Conrad explores the meanings of his Congo experience and the sociopolitical movements of his time. The advent of Marlow, Conrad's "inner" narrator in "Youth" and "Heart of Darkness" and *Lord Jim* (and later, in *Chance*) will help to resolve some of the metaphorical inconsistencies and difficulties of point of view that plague the *Nigger.* Conrad will work toward a greater realism of values and a more closely controlled, ironic style; and despite the decline of his final years, his fiction generally will display a deepening self-awareness and an advancing technical growth. But *The Nigger of the "Narcissus"* can never lose its importance for those readers who believe that art finds its ultimate justification both in its esthetic integrity and in the breadth and seriousness of its ethical appeal.

The Nigger of the "Narcissus": A Re-examination

by James E. Miller, Jr.

It is surely true, as Percy Lubbock once pointed out,[1] that before a critic can talk about the technique, he must first discover what a novel is *about:* if he cannot reduce the subject to graspable proportions, if he cannot state it in a few phrases or sentences, then he has nothing to which he can relate and in terms of which he can evaluate the technique. An isolated technical device, a particular symbol or a special style, has no worth as such, but is valuable or not *only* in its relevance to the novel's center. The first important question, then, which must be answered about *Nigger* is, What is it about? To say that it is about a six months' voyage of the *Narcissus* is to place the subject on so general a level that almost anything is admissible, almost nothing irrelevant: it is no more about the *Narcissus* than it is about the sea; Conrad indicated that the ship and the sea were subordinate, even dispensable, when he said that *Nigger* was concerned not with a problem of the sea but rather with "a problem that has arisen on board a ship where the conditions of complete isolation from all land entanglements make it stand out with particular force and colouring." [2] Nor is the novel about the Nigger, James Wait, for, as Conrad

---

"The Nigger of the 'Narcissus': A Re-examination," by James E. Miller, Jr. Reprinted by permission of the Modern Language Association from PMLA, LXVI (December 1951), 911–18. © 1951 by The Modern Language Association of America. The first two paragraphs, which briefly review criticism of the Nigger to 1951, have been omitted.

[1] *The Craft of Fiction* (New York: Peter Smith, 1945), p. 41: "A subject, one and whole and irreducible—a novel cannot begin to take shape till it has this for its support. It seems obvious; yet there is nothing more familiar to a novel reader of today than the difficulty of discovering what the novel in his hand is about. What was the novelist's intention, in a phrase?"

[2] Conrad, *Life and Letters*, by G. Jean-Aubry (New York: Doubleday & Company, Inc., 1927), II, 342.

tells us in his preface, "in the book he is nothing; he is merely the centre of the ship's collective psychology and the pivot of the action" (p. ix).[3] It would be difficult to propose Wait as the central character especially in view of the storm in the third chapter, which supplants him temporarily as a dominant influence on the crew.

There is no central character in the novel, as Conrad's statement above suggests: it is the crew, collectively, that occupies the center of the novel. But Conrad is not concerned with everything that happens to the crew on board the *Narcissus* (such a catalogue of events, if not impossible, would surely not make a novel); more precisely, he is concerned with tracing a change that takes place in the crew: in general terms, the crew passes from ignorance to knowledge about life and about death; as a result, and more specifically, the transition in the crew is from diversity to solidarity. It is on this change that Conrad focuses our attention, and it is within the terms of this change that he constructs his symbols, and it is the drama of this change that *is* the structure of the novel. A brief glance at the opening and close of *Nigger* bears out the central importance of this transition. As the novel opens, it is night, and our attention is directed to the forecastle: "A hum of voices was heard there, while port and starboard, in the illuminated doorways, silhouettes of moving men appeared for a moment, very black, without relief, like figures cut out of sheet tin" (p. 3). It is, indeed, as a "clash of voices and cries" that the crew, a diverse group of many nationalities, first appears to us. In the final pages of the novel, one striking sentence pictures the crew for us in very different terms: "The dark knot of seamen drifted in sunshine" (p. 172). The crew has, in the progress of the novel, passed out of the darkness of ignorance into the light of wisdom; it has changed from clashing diversity into the peaceful solidarity of a "knot." And the closing lines of the novel suggest the significance of the experience the crew has undergone: "Haven't we, together and upon the immortal sea, wrung out a meaning from our sinful lives?" (p. 173).

To discover this meaning is to discover the knowledge which the crew gained on its voyage on the *Narcissus*. Perhaps the knowledge can best be explained in terms of the dominant symbols of the book (at the risk, of course, of oversimplification): James Wait and the sea, as symbols of death and life; Singleton and Donkin, as symbols of opposed attitudes toward death and life. The significance that James Wait is to have in the novel and the attitude of the crew toward him

[3] [Page references here are to Doubleday, Doran's 1945 edition of the *Nigger*, which reprints Conrad's Foreword to the first American edition. Pagination of the text is identical with that of other major Dent and Doubleday editions.]

as symbol are shadowed forth in the opening chapter, in a brief scene constructed around the ambiguity of Wait's name:

> The distinct and motionless group stirred, broke up, began to move forward.
> "Wait!" cried a deep, ringing voice.
> All stood still (p. 17).

The electrifying command of the voice and name instil in the crew that uneasiness with which it is to be plagued throughout the book. The ambiguity becomes reality in the second chapter, when the crew comes to know Wait for what he is, death in disguise: "A black mist emanated from him; a subtle and dismal influence; a something cold and gloomy that floated out and settled on all the faces like a mourning veil" (p. 34).

As the crew is to take its lesson of death from James Wait, so it is to take its lesson of life from the sea. The mysterious, enigmatical, and immortal sea comes to violent life in the third chapter; in a very real sense, it *becomes* life for the moment and gives the crew a vision of itself that is the sum of wisdom:

> On men reprieved by its disdainful mercy, the immortal sea confers in its justice the full privilege of desired unrest. Through the perfect wisdom of its grace they are not permitted to meditate at ease upon the complicated and acrid savour of existence. They must without pause justify their life to the eternal pity that commands toil to be hard and unceasing, from sunrise to sunset, from sunset to sunrise; till the weary succession of nights and days tainted by the obstinate clamour of sages, demanding bliss and an empty heaven, is redeemed at last by the vast silence of pain and labour, by the dumb fear and the dumb courage of men obscure, forgetful, and enduring (p. 90).

Closely related to these symbols are Donkin and Singleton, who represent opposed attitudes toward death and life, attitudes which vie with each other to dominate the crew. Donkin is introduced to us as "the man that cannot steer, that cannot splice, that dodges the work on dark nights . . . the man who curses the sea while the others work. . . . [He] knows nothing of courage, of endurance, and of the unexpressed faith, of the unspoken loyalty that knits together a ship's company" (pp. 10–11). Donkin thus becomes ignorance personified, just as old Singleton is "the incarnation of barbarian wisdom." Unfortunately, Singleton is the last of an unremembered, unsung race: "The men who could understand his silence were gone—those men who knew how to exist beyond the pale of life and within sight of eternity. They had been strong, as those are strong who know neither doubts nor hopes" (p. 25).

Donkin and Singleton (the names themselves are suggestive: Donkin connotes that stupidest of animals, while Singleton connotes integrity, solidarity) are the two poles between which the crew vacillates. Donkin in his sneaking attitude toward death (James Wait) and in his cowardly attitude toward life (the sea), represents the ultimate in that ignorance from which the crew eventually passes to the primitive wisdom of Singleton, as exhibited in his contrasting courageous acceptance of death and life for what they are. Thus Conrad brings back to life the race of men, Singleton's comrades, which he at first told us was extinct, for the men of the *Narcissus* at the end of its voyage do know "toil, privation, violence, debauchery—but [know] not fear, and [have] no desire of spite in their hearts."

And what is this primitive wisdom which the crew possesses at the end of its voyage? It is important first to see what it is not: "He [James Wait] was demoralising. Through him we were becoming highly humanised, tender, complex, excessively decadent: we understood the subtlety of his fear, sympathised with all his repulsions, shrinkings, evasions, delusions—as though we had been overcivilised, and rotten, and without any knowledge of the meaning of life" (p. 139). This "knowledge of the meaning of life" is not a sophisticated, complex, highly civilized or civilizing (in the usual sense) knowledge; it is, rather, a basic insight into fundamental, primitive truths. It is, first, a view of life which results not so much in an understanding as in an attitude of acceptance. Life *is* toil, *is* privation, *is* violence, as only the sea can prove; and it is not man's place to doubt or shrink from these hard facts of life, any more than it is his place to doubt or shrink from the mysterious sea. He must acknowledge and accept them with courage. But the wisdom is also a wisdom of death. It is this insight that Singleton has in the midst of the voyage of the *Narcissus:* "He looked upon the immortal sea with the awakened and groping perception of its heartless might; he saw it unchanged, black and foaming under the eternal scrutiny of the stars; he heard its impatient voice calling for him out of a pitiless vastness full of unrest, of turmoil, and of terror. He looked far upon it, and he saw an immensity tormented and blind, moaning and furious, that claimed all the days of his tenacious life, and, when life was over, would claim the worn-out body of its slave" (p. 94). Singleton's wisdom has been completed; his vision of life has been extended to a vision of death, death as inexplicable, inevitable, to be accepted with the same courage with which life has been accepted. This primitive wisdom of life and death, which the crew is to possess by the end of the voyage, is, as Conrad tells us in his preface, the source of solidarity, "the solidarity in mysterious origin, in toil, in joy, in hope, in uncertain fate, which binds men to each other and all mankind to the visible world" (p. xiv). The "knot" which binds the crew at the end of *Nigger* is, indeed, a sailor's knot, tied with a sailor's wisdom.

The structure of *Nigger* is essentially dramatic. Suspense is achieved through the juxtaposition of two probabilities: the one probability is that the crew will turn to Singleton, achieve his wisdom; the other is that the crew will be persuaded by Donkin to accept his attitude, his ignorance. Although neither of the probabilities is ever absent, one or the other is always dominant. It is here that Conrad's selection is apparent, and it is here that his chapter divisions take on significance. For Conrad has selected, arranged, and represented his events so that the dominant probability shifts from chapter to chapter; but, in addition to this alternation there is also an ascending order of intensity of the probabilities until the climax in the one is reached when the crew is brought to almost open rebellion by Donkin and the climax in the other is reached when the sight of land brings Jimmy's death (proving Singleton infallible in his primitive logic) and the crew through the voice of Belfast, shouts its new-found wisdom to the reluctant dead: "Jimmy, be a man!"

The central incident of the first chapter is the mustering of the crew, which enables Conrad to introduce to us in a somewhat systematic way the real protagonist of his story, the crew (just as, at the end of the novel, the device of the paying-off enables him to bring the individual members of the crew before the reader's eye once more for a last glimpse). Both lines of probability are established. Although the crew spots Donkin for what he is, he knows "how to conquer the naive instincts of that crowd." But it is Singleton as symbol that dominates the chapter, which, significantly, ends with the long description of his now forgotten shipmates of the past, the "everlasting children of the mysterious sea."

In Chapter Two, however, the dominant symbol shifts. The crew, in its doubts and uneasiness about the newly discovered omnipresent companion of James Wait, goes to old Singleton for advice. The oracle hands down his decision, "Why, of course he will die," and the crew has something definite to which to cling—but only for a moment, for Donkin is quick to twist and make meaningless the oracle's words, and the crew, easily persuaded, begins to hate Singleton. Wisdom is pitted against ignorance, and ignorance, for the moment, is triumphant. Donkin's attitude toward Wait (or death) prevails, and its disruption of the peaceful life of the ship is detailed in the final lines of the chapter: "He [Wait] overshadowed the ship. Invulnerable in his promise of speedy corruption he trampled on our self-respect, he demonstrated to us daily our want of moral courage: he tainted our lives" (p. 47).

But, as the crew had at first reckoned without Donkin, so Donkin had reckoned without the sea. Donkin's triumph is short-lived, for again, in Chapter Three, symbol is pitted against symbol, and wisdom comes off best. In the struggle to survive the furious storm, in the struggle to free James Wait from his death-trap, in the struggle to right the ship, Donkin is conspicuously absent, Singleton quietly but courageously fulfilling his duty. It is natural that there would follow from the crew contempt for the cowardly Donkin and respect for the steadfast Singleton. An image which seems to sum up the whole of Singleton's wisdom closes yet dominates our memory of the entire chapter: "He steered with care" (p. 89).

The "perfect wisdom," however, which the sea has so generously conferred and which Singleton has so admirably demonstrated, is not easily remembered. In Chapter Four, Donkin skulks about, sowing the seeds of dissension: "We abominated the creature and could not deny the luminous truth of his contentions" (p. 101). When the Captain, attempting to play along with the Nigger's great pretence, orders Wait to remain in his cabin, Donkin seizes the opportunity, his last great chance, to stir the men to the point of open revolt. In the confusion that follows Donkin's throwing of the belaying pin, in the midst of the muttering and rebellious men, Singleton stands "monumental, indistinct." It is at this climactic point that the two symbols at war with each other come face to face: "Singleton peered downwards with puzzled attention, as though he couldn't find him.—'Damn you!' he said, vaguely, giving it up" (p. 130). "Unspeakable" wisdom cannot communicate with unfathomable ignorance. It is with an ambiguous silence that, the next morning, the crew watches the Captain dress down Donkin; but Donkin's influence has already passed its greatest height.

It is not, however, until, in the last chapter, after Jimmy's death, that the crew sees the folly of its false attitude toward the Nigger alive and, confronted by the proof of his prophecies come true, penetrates to the primitive wisdom of old Singleton. The courage it could not give Jimmy alive it attempts to instil in him in death. Only Donkin is absent at Jimmy's funeral. He has not only been "judged and cast out by the august silence of [the immortal sea's] might," but, after the ship has reached port, and the men are being paid off for the voyage, when he invites his shipmates for a drink (to be paid for with Jimmy's money), "no one moved. There was a silence; a silence of blank faces and stony looks" (p. 170). The rejection of Donkin's ignorance is finally complete, and Singleton's primitive wisdom is at last triumphant. The crew has passed from diversity based on ignorance through a false unity based on the lie perpetrated by Donkin, to, finally, the true "knot" of solidarity based on genuine insight into the meaning of life and death. It has become the kind of crew that Singleton had known in his youth.

The style of *Nigger* has received a kind of praise that is in reality damning to the work as a whole; it has been assumed that the cadence and the implicit meanings of the highly metaphorical language have some value which bear very little or no relation to the "story" or to the center of the novel. Almost any page offers abundant examples of the richness of Conrad's style:

> At night, through the impenetrable darkness of earth and heaven, broad sheets of flame waved noiselessly; and for half a second the becalmed craft stood out with its masts and rigging, with every sail and every rope distinct and black in the centre of a fiery outburst, like a charred ship enclosed in a globe of fire. And, again, for long hours she remained lost in a vast universe of night and silence where gentle sighs wandering here and there like forlorn souls, made the still sails flutter as in sudden fear, and the ripple of a beshrouded ocean whisper its compassion afar—in a voice mournful, immense, and faint . . . (p 104).

The imagery here, as throughout the book, is not decorative but functional: at the very heart of the novel is the search for meaning, the search for wisdom; the words seem to explore the scene, the sea, the universe in search of that meaning and wisdom. And if the crew is supposed to achieve wisdom in its voyage on the *Narcissus,* is not the reader also meant to receive a "glimpse of truth" in his voyage with Conrad? The "magic suggestiveness" of the style is not mere superficial trimming: it probes beneath the surfaces for those insights which are to bring the crew (and perhaps the reader) the primitive, the fundamental wisdom of life and death.

Trial by Water: Joseph Conrad's
The Nigger of the "Narcissus"

by Vernon Young

> Both men and ships live in an unstable element, are subject
> to subtle and powerful influences, and want to have their
> merits understood rather than their faults found out.
>
> —Conrad: *The Mirror of the Sea*

> I have no doubt that star-gazing is a fine occupation, for it
> leads you within the borders of the unattainable. But map-
> gazing, to which I became addicted so early, brings the prob-
> lems of the great spaces of the earth into stimulating and
> direct contact with sane curiosity and gives an honest precision
> to one's imaginative faculty.
>
> —Conrad: "Geography and Some Ex-
> plorers" in *Last Essays*

The Nigger of the "Narcissus" is the account of a sailing ship's
voyage from Bombay to London by the way of the Cape, during
which the ship nearly founders with all hands and the crew is
temporarily demoralized by the presence of a Negro seaman named
James Wait. The Negro dies and is buried at sea; the *Narcissus* arrives in London with no further incident. *The Nigger of the "Narcissus"* is a study of character on trial, a memorial to seafarers under
sail, together with disclaimers of those who would have undermined
the innocence and pertinacity of their toil. *The Nigger of the "Narcissus"* is an allegory of temptation and endurance, a microcosm of
the moral world of relationships and responsibilities. And since, as

in all myth, principles as well as patterns of action are reiterated across space and time, the social motif of *The Nigger of the "Narcissus"* is referable to the individual psyche, and the novel, under this aspect, is an adventure of the soul.

It is the third aspect, the mythic, never openly acknowledged by Conrad himself, which gives to the novel its vibratory temper and its perennial interest. Conrad's fraternal loyalty to the nautical facts of the case is finally subordinate to his transcendental theme, fortified throughout the novel by its equivalence in symbolic action. Geography and meteorology combine with crises of human conduct and with analogues of the metaphysical cycle to produce a rich complex of correspondences.

The *Narcissus,* then, sails from Bombay to London—which is to say, from the East (source, for Conrad, of the exotic and the ominous) to the capital of the mercantile West. The voyage, a routine "homeward passage," necessitates the traversal of 60° southward to attain 20° northward; to reach home port, the *Narcissus* must sail away from it, so to speak, down miles of longitude against the West Wind Drift and around the cape of storms called Good Hope, before she can straighten north and sail directly home with assisting trade winds. The crucial calamity—the deadly plunge of the ship on to her *port* side (the left, or sinister, side)—and the termination of the power which may be said to have effected it, the death of the Nigger, occur equidistantly from the Zero Line (the equator of day and night), approximately 40° south and 40° north, respectively. Mercator's Projection thus becomes a corollary graph of the crew's spiritual ordeal.

Leaving one continent for another, the *Narcissus* sails *out of* darkness, *into* darkness, since Conrad's moral geography was opposite in value to Herman Melville's, for example. The sea, "the unstable element," was, to Conrad, the amniotic ocean of life, itself: like life uncertain, incalculable but enchanting and worthier of men's challenge than the land. In all Conrad's novels, the land is the home of the enemy. The jungle, the forest, the city: these are his symbols of treachery. The sea, however disastrous or inclement it may become, is as neutral and as irrefutable as the life-cycle; it is the given, if "destructive element." [1] and in the face of it man's duty is, like Singleton's in the novel, to "steer with care."

---

[1] This phrase from *Lord Jim* was radically misemployed by Stephen Spender (in *The Destructive Element,* 1935), following the lead of I. A. Richards, and criticism since has largely accepted the misinterpretation. To reread the passage closely in the knowledge of Conrad's Neptunian bias is to discover, with Crankshaw, that "the

Conrad's earliest fictional commitments to the antipodal character of land and sea are underlined in this novel. The land lies "within the frontier of infamy and filth, within that border of dirt and hunger, of misery and dissipation, that comes down on all sides to the water's edge of the incorruptible ocean . . ." The *Narcissus,* a creature of light, was born in darkness, "in black eddies of smoke, under a grey sky, on the banks of the Clyde. The clamorous and sombre stream gives birth to things of beauty that float away into the sunshine of the world to be loved by men." When she leaves Bombay with her yards hoisted she becomes "a high and lonely pyramid, gliding all shining and white, through the sunlit mist. The tug turned short round and went away towards the land [resembling] an enormous and aquatic black beetle, surprised by the light, overwhelmed by the sunshine, trying to escape with ineffectual effort into the distant gloom of the land . . ." [2] Upon arrival in the Thames at the end of the voyage, the *Narcissus* reenters the cloud: "the shadows of soulless walls fell upon her, the dust of all the continents leaped upon her deck, and a swarm of strange men, clambering up her sides, took possession of her in the name of the sordid earth. She had ceased to live."

Wait, the Negro, originally a product of the jungle, one supposes —he is specifically alluded to as a West Indian, enforcing the equation of West and Death—is, with Donkin, "the independent offspring of the ignoble freedom of the slums full of disdain and hate for the austere servitude of the sea," set off against the Able Seaman, Singleton, who, in forty-five years, has lived no more than forty months ashore. The narrator's final reflection on the crew recapitulates this sheep-and-goats distinction. "I never saw them again . . . Singleton has no doubt taken with him the long record of his faithful work into the peaceful depths of an hospitable sea. And Donkin, who never did a decent day's work in his life, no doubt earns his living by discoursing with filthy eloquence upon the right of labor to live. So be it! Let the earth and the sea each have its own."

By not accepting the moral dichotomy of land and sea as a highly

---

destructive element" equals, not the chaos of experience, and a "state of complete unbelief" (Spender), but rather the normative and traditional element of being. "The way is to the destructive element submit yourself. . . . If [a man] tries to climb out into the air . . . he drowns." In this figure, the *air* should be the destructive element by Spender's interpretation.

[2] The antithesis here is unquestionably a sidelong glance at the Egyptian figure of the pyramid, prime symbol of direction and sun-worship, and of the scarab, symbol of creative energy.

charged metaphor, the reader of *The Nigger of the "Narcissus"* might well accuse Conrad of sentimental sophistry; accepting it, he will be in a position to appreciate how effectively it is cofeatured with the other symbolic properties—particularly with the permeating use of color contrasts. White and black, pink or blue and black, light and shade, sun and cloud, gold and darkness—within the total form, these oppositions are vitally operative, usually accompanied by relative variations of weather. So much is this tonality the index to Conrad's alignment of moods and forces that its most pertinent appearances are well worth isolating before taking up considerations less purely visual.

II

Among other possible reasons for preferring the finally established title to earlier ones (among which were *The Forecastle: A Tale of Ships* and *Men and Children of the Sea: A Tale of the Forecastle*), Conrad surely felt the force of the black and white dualism, while taking advantage, perhaps, of the British association of narcissus with death, thereby giving a paradoxical twist to the pairing of skull and blossom, root and flower.[3] In any case, the title indubitably sets the key which is sounded in the very first sentence:

> Mr. Baker, chief mate of the ship *Narcissus,* stepped in one stride out of his lighted cabin into the darkness of the quarterdeck.

When the Negro, Wait, joins the ship,

> He held his head up in the glare of the lamp—a head vigorously modelled into deep shadows and shining lights . . .

After he retires, groaning, to his bunk in the forecastle,

> Singleton stood at the door with his face to the light and his back to the darkness.

(This vignette, sharpening here the presence of Wait, reverberates long after in one of the most remarkable sentences in the book when,

[3] The fact of there having been an actual ship, *Narcissus,* and an actual Wait in Conrad's seafaring experience is of course less important than his retention of the facts he could artistically transmute. The possible bearing of the old *Narcissus* legend I but hesitantly advance. The sea certainly *reflects* the collective moral features of the crew: ". . . the sea knew all, and would in time infallibly unveil to each the wisdom hidden in all the errors, the certitude that lurks in doubts." This mirror tests the vanity of all aboard, but I have no wish to urge the image beyond reasonable evidence for its fitness; notoriously, symbols have a life of their own.

at the end of the voyage, the older man steps up to the shipping office pay table:

> Singleton came up, venerable—and uncertain as to daylight; . . . his hands, that never hesitated in the great light of the open sea, could hardly find the small pile of gold in the profound darkness of the shore.)

During the voyage, every climax of weather as well as every dramatic position in which Wait figures is similarly balanced. Emerging from the forecastle, Wait

> seemed to hasten the retreat of departing light by his very presence; the setting sun dipped sharply, as though fleeing before our nigger. . . .

As the men struggle to extricate Wait from behind the bulkhead while the ship is capsizing,

> in the sunshiny blue square of the door, the boatswain's face, bearded and dark, Wamibo's face, wild and pale, hung over—watching. . . .

As they are crossing the equator, when the influence of Wait has settled into its most oppressive effects,

> The invisible sun, sweeping above the upright masts, made on the clouds a blurred stain of rayless light, and a similar patch of faded radiance kept pace with it from east to west over the unglittering level of the waters. At night, through the impenetrable darkness of earth and heaven, broad sheets of flame waved noiselessly; and for half a second the becalmed craft stood out with its masts and rigging, with every sail and every rope distinct and black in the centre of a fiery outburst, like a charred ship enclosed in a globe of fire.

(The ship on the line of the equator and the square-rigging against the sky form a monogram of a fiery cross.) Concurrent with the dead calm after land is first sighted, Wait, attended by Donkin, lies dying in the deckhouse. His last words are

> "Light . . . the lamp . . . and . . . go."

Donkin, after stealing Wait's money is

> . . . just in time to see Wait's eyes blaze up and go out at once, like two lamps overturned together by a sweeping blow. . . . [Outside] sleeping men, huddled under jackets, made on the lighted deck shapeless dark mounds that had the appearance of neglected graves. . . . The ship slept. And the immortal sea stretched away, immense and hazy, like the image of life, with a glittering surface and lightless depths.

The coda that follows the marine burial of Wait is brisk and lambent; the prose throws off saltatory images of light which conquer those of darkness (and which, incidentally, involve an energetic sequence of "pathetic fallacy"):

> . . . the clouds swifter than the ship, more free, but without a home. The coast to welcome her stepped out of space into the sunshine. The lofty headlands trod masterfully into the sea; the wide bays smiled in the light. . . . At night the headlands retreated, the bays advanced into one unbroken line of gloom. The lights of earth mingled with the lights of heaven; and above the tossing lanterns of a trawling fleet a great light-house shone steadily, like an enormous riding light burning above a vessel of fabulous dimensions.

The *Narcissus* is berthed and her men are "scattered by the dissolving contact with land." The narrator last sees them, their pockets full of money,

> swaying irresolute and noisy on the broad flagstones before the Mint. They were bound for the Black Horse, where men, in fur caps with brutal faces and in shirt sleeves, dispense out of varnished barrels the illusions of strength. . . .

A concluding ambience balances the earliest view of the men as they had mustered on deck in Bombay:

> The dark knot of seamen drifted in sunshine. . . . The sunshine of heaven fell like a gift of grace on the mud of the earth, on the remembering and mute stones, on greed, selfishness. . . . And to the right of the dark group the stained front of the Mint, cleansed by the flood of light, stood for a moment dazzling and white like a marble palace in a fairy tale. The crew of the *Narcissus* drifted out of sight.

The reader will discover for himself many more such images than I have thought necessary to display here: these are perhaps sufficient to verify Conrad's purposive employment of them. It will have been seen that although these dark-and-light oppositions mainly express conventional connotations of death and life, evil and good (land and sea, left and right), there are moments when they represent no such clear antimony. White hail streaming from a black cloud, the dark boatswain against the bright blue door, a "withered" moon, and others, are clearly not intended to be consistent with the moral polarities conveyed by the general thematic continuity; they are simply part of an absorption in tonal antithesis. In the superb sentence of the gold in the darkness of the shore, gold and darkness are not opposed but correlated, morally speaking—as they are again in that extraordinary touch of the men going from the light-flooded Mint to the Black

Horse. This oblique manipulation of symbols may be better appreciated in the light of a statement on cinematic art, which, as Edward Crankshaw was first among critics to point out, Conrad's art so often resembled. Writing on the subject of cinematic color values, Sergei Eisenstein declared, in *The Film Sense:*

> In art it is not the *absolute* relationships that are decisive, but those *arbitrary* relationships within a system of images dictated by the particular work of art. . . . the *emotional intelligibility* and function of color will rise from the natural order of establishing *the color imagery of the work, coincidental with the process of shaping the living movement of the whole work.*

III

In *The Nigger of the "Narcissus,"* what Conrad's imagery substantiates above all is the apocalyptic nature of the novel's outline. The four Empedoclean elements, the polar variants of night and day, hell and heaven, West and East, encompass the cosmological pyramid which is the subject. In "the living movement of the whole," Conrad's symbolism subscribes to no single order of religious values; it synthesizes universally recurring emblems in man's expression of his destiny and places them at the service of the novel's contingent subject, the moral effects of illusion.

> The true peace of God begins at any spot a thousand miles from the nearest land; and when he sends there the messengers of his might it is not in terrible wrath against crime, presumption and folly, but paternally, to chasten simple hearts—ignorant hearts that know nothing of life, and beat undisturbed by envy or greed.

An exaggerated reassertion of oceanic felicity, this paragraph is also the nuclear designation of the *Narcissus'* voyage as a trial by water, not so much to initiate as to chasten, to test the illusion of invulnerability which each man wears in varying proportion. The primary agent of this trial is the Nigger, James Wait. "I belong to the ship," is his calm announcement to the chief mate as he stands muster. In the occult vocabulary he would be described as an *elemental,* a servant of the general law of nature; from the psychological bias, he is an embodiment of the subconscious, instinctual but regressive quality in man. Twentieth-century anthropology, to say nothing of sociology, has perhaps diminished, if not discredited, for most of us, the spell of the lurid, the mysterious or the evil in the person of the Negro, but it would be a mistake to see in James Wait only an exercise of Conradian chauvinism. Conrad's experience with African backcountry savages certainly justified his using the type as illustrative of the black-magical and the unevolved. When describing Wait's face as "pathetic and brutal: the tragic, the mysterious, the repulsive mask of a nigger's soul," he was enjoying the privilege, apparently inevitable to their psychology, which the white races have taken upon themselves, of seeing the dark races as either exotic or sinister, but in any case inferior.

Metaphysically, Wait serves a purpose comparable to that of El Negro in Melville's "Benito Cereno": he is the *spirit* of blackness, archetype of the unknown forces from the depths. With this important difference, however: he is not sensationally demonic but, rather, insidious and emanating. His role is a rehearsal, in Conrad's literature, of that "barbarous and superb woman" in "Heart of Darkness" who, as the steamboat leaves with the damned and moribund remains of Kurtz, stretches "tragically her bare arms after [them] over the sombre and glittering river." Wait, by a form of adjuration less explicit, more accessible to the gullibility of simple men, all but deprives the crew of their will to live. Consentient with the natural perils that haunt its progress, he accompanies the *Narcissus* across the waters of strife, casting his spell on the probity of the crew's endeavors.

A symbol of postponement, his name is cardinal token: Wait. Conrad plays upon it when the Nigger belatedly joins the ship, shouting "Wait" to the astonished officer who takes the word as an insolent injunction rather than as a name. Wait's burial at sea reemphasizes the tenacity of his inertia, for when the plank is first raised to slide his body overboard, he holds fast until one of the sailors, after screaming "Jimmy, be a man! . . . Go, Jimmy . . . ," gives the corpse needed impetus with a light push.[4] But *Wait* has also, by virtue of the Nigger's retarding and oppressive action, the force of the other spelling, *weight*. (Immediately following his plummet from the deck, "The ship rolled as if relieved of an unfair burden.") From his bed-ridden vantage point, supine and seemingly helpless, he drags on the initial resistance of the men like an anchor, beguiles their sympathy, gradually vitiates their resolution by the pathos of his induced condition. (Naturalistically, his eventual death may be construed as psychogenic.) His appeal is to the slacker in each man's heart, awakening the desire to rebel, abandonment of duty, and the luxury of irresponsible rest.

[4] Conrad later discloses that the boatswain had forgotten to grease the plank and that the carpenter had left a protruding nail—a somewhat vulgar irony, one must admit, to safeguard his fear of wholesale commitment to the irrational.

The near undoing of the crew is the result of their returning good for evil, a practice which, in extremity, was to Conrad a sin of pride. As he wrote in a letter to Marguerite Poradowska,

> . . . to return good for evil is not only profoundly immoral but dangerous, in that it sharpens the appetite for evil in the malevolent and develops (perhaps unconsciously) that latent tendency towards hypocrisy in the . . . let us say, benevolent.

Similarly to Lingard in Conrad's Almayer novels, the crew of the *Narcissus* become victims of benevolent egotism, and their sponsorship, like Lingard's, is betrayed. Wait meets their compassion with abuse; he flaunts his death-urge before their living eyes.

> He fascinated us. He would never let doubt die. He overshadowed the ship. Invulnerable in his promise of speedy corruption he trampled on our self-respect, he demonstrated to us daily our want of moral courage; he tainted our lives.

The determining incident of their slavery occurs when they rescue Wait from the deckhouse in which he is trapped by the storm; though he insults them for their pains, they are more than ever in his power. They come to exemplify the negative hazard involved in the young Lingard's Oriental sentiment that "When you save people from death you take a share in their life."

In the oblique hours of rescue, they have been on a very long journey toward oblivion.

> The return on the poop was like the return of wanderers after many years amongst people marked by the desolation of time.[5]

They have undergone the first trial, entered the dominion of death and been reborn; the salvage of Wait effects a respite, a temporary release from danger, in the manner of the old tales in which an ogre was freed from a cave, a witch from an oak-tree, or an imp from a bottle. Freedom is gained only by entering into closer bondage with the genie.[6] The weather clears, the sea is calmed.

---

[5] Note the similarity of Donkin's return from his nocturnal vigil with the dying Nigger: ". . . as though he had expected to find the men dead, familiar things gone for ever: as though, like a wanderer returning after many years, he had expected to see bewildering changes."

[6] In *The Hero with a Thousand Faces* (Pantheon-Bollingen, 1949, pp. 69ff.), Joseph Campbell discusses the role of the supernatural helper in the monomyth. This helper, often a guide or supporter, may be dangerous, "the lurer of the innocent soul into realms of trial," sometimes signifying "the inscrutability of the guide that we are following, to the peril of all our rational ends."

> . . . from that time our life seemed to start afresh as though we had
> died and had been resuscitated. All the first part of the voyage, the
> Indian Ocean on the other side of the Cape, all that was lost in a haze,
> like an ineradicable suspicion of some previous existence.

The more extreme test is to follow. Their solidarity with the defect-
ing Negro established by their plucking him to safety, the crew members arise to articulate discontent when Wait finally offers to turn to
with the men and his services are refused by Captain Allistoun, who is
privately convinced that the Nigger is indeed going to die. The fatally
deluded allegiance of the men will not let them believe this. No
longer able to distinguish the smell of mortality, they offer their disbelief to Wait as a propitiation, as if he were the totem, the cult-object
of a primitive clan. "The desolation of time" has obliterated their
etiological powers and returned them to the rudimentary form of
communal belief through contagion (for which Emil Durkheim has
provided the term *surexcitation*).

As it becomes unmistakably evident that Wait will die and his
"fleshless head" resembles "a disinterred black skull," disbelief changes
to anxiety. And, as Singleton has predicted, Wait dies after land is
sighted; the reaction is one of sullen surprise.

> We did not know till then how much faith we had put in his delusions.
> We had taken his chances of life so much at his own valuation that his
> death, like the death of an old belief, shook the foundations of our soci-
> ety. A common bond was gone; the strong, effective and respectable bond
> of a sentimental lie.

Wait is stitched into a canvas and dropped overboard into the "lightless depths"—to starboard, toward the East, the night, the land,
and the direction of rebirth.

IV

The men of the *Narcissus* are modified by James Wait in accord
with the drift of their respective temperaments. The trial by water
corroborates either the virtue or the ignoble fallacy of their necessary
illusions. Captain Allistoun is never for a moment intimidated by
Jimmy's malingering. He it is who keeps his head when the *Narcissus*
heels and the carpenter, in a panic, grabs an ax with which to cut
the masts free. Allistoun forbids the action, thereby saving all hands.
While the half-drowned men cling to the canted deck, waiting for
death, he remains on the poop, eyes ahead for the first opportunity

to shout "wear ship." (On the analogy of the psychic organism, Allistoun is the *superego,* dominating consciously the subterranean murmurs of defeat. His insistence that Wait remain in his cabin is a further act of will over the emerging death-wish; he refuses it the light of day.) The last order he gives to the officer on leaving the ship summarizes his supreme rationality: "Don't forget to wind up the chronometers tomorrow morning."

Singleton, in less authoritative measure, is the Captain's moral counterpart in the forecastle. A singleton is an independent card in a suit; whether or not Conrad chose this association, the name is, in any case, a reflection of the sailor's forthright characteristic: single tone.

> Singleton lived untouched by human emotions. Taciturn and unsmiling, he breathed among us—in that alone resembling the rest of the crowd.

He is heavily tattooed and is first introduced as "the incarnation of barbarian wisdom serene in the blasphemous turmoil of the world." The simplicity of Singleton's candor is the exact countercheck to the simplicity of the Nigger's deceit: the sea and the jungle. Less than a week after leaving Bombay, Singleton meets the Negro's foul misanthropy with the disconcertingly direct question, "Are you dying?" During the Cape disaster he remains braced at the wheel and, in common with the others, derives from the experience its lesson for his own identity. Charley, the youngest of the crew, is "subdued by the sudden disclosure of the insignificance of his youth"; "Singleton was possessed of sinister truth . . . the cook of fame—."

The "sinister truth" is Singleton's recognition of his mortality.

> Old! . . . like a man bound treacherously while he sleeps, he woke up fettered by the long chain of disregarded years.

His indifference to Wait's corruption is born not of rational understanding but of fearlessness bred from experience and from a simple set of convictions little different from belief in magic (white magic— he signs his name with a cross). Singleton and the cook, together, represent the veracity that sometimes lurks in inherited superstition. Singleton's naive science of cause and effect is certainly not refuted by the circumstance that Jimmy *does* die in sight of land and that wind *does* rise after his submersion.

Podmore, the religious fanatic, is scorned by the Captain and the embarrassed men alike, but he is, nonetheless, the cook—their nourisher. While they sprawl helplessly on the toppling ship, only Podmore has the imagination to sense their position in relation to eternity. After

serving the men from the water-cask, he sits to leeward and shouts back
to the men's congratulations,

> . . . but the seas were breaking in thunder just then, and we only caught
> snatches that sounded like: "Providence" and "born again."

Podmore braves the diluvial decks to reach the galley and incredibly
makes coffee for the crew.

> Afterwards Archie declared that the thing was "meeraculous" . . . and
> we did our best to conceal our admiration under the wit of fine irony.
> The cook rebuked our levity, declaring himself, with solemn animation,
> to have been the object of a special mercy for the saving of our unholy
> lives. . . .

While Wait slips toward death, the men's unbelief is reproved by
Podmore's fatuous exaltation at the hope of saving the Negro's soul.
He is momentarily inspired:

> He saw flowing garments, clean-shaved faces, a sea of light,—a lake of
> pitch. . . . He had prayerfully divested himself of the last vestige of
> his humanity. He was a voice—a fleshless and sublime thing, as on that
> memorable night—the night when he went walking over the sea to make
> coffee for perishing sinners.

Enraptured and preposterous Podmore may be, but his certainty
that the Nigger's soul is possessed by the Devil is closer to the spiritual
nexus of experience than the callous nescience of men like Donkin.
The crew members in general never do understand the moral meaning of James Wait. But the cool rationality of Allistoun, the intuitive wisdom of Singleton, and the overheated zeal of Podmore
discover, behind the mask of a dying shirker, the infrahuman visage
of the Satanic.

Donkin, the Cockney, is the lowest common denominator, the
eternal and omnipresent grumbler, a thing of rags and patches with
no soul of his own. He feeds on other men's identities as he wears
their cast-off clothes. At the beginning of the voyage, he appears in
the forecastle, truculent, half-naked, squealing of his "rights."

> He knew how to conquer the naive instincts of that crowd. In a moment
> they gave him their compassion, jocularly, contemptuously, or surlily;
> and at first it took the shape of a blanket thrown at him as he stood there
> with the white skin of his limbs showing his human kinship through
> the black fantasy of his rags. Then a pair of old shoes fell at his muddy
> feet. . . . The gust of their benevolence sent a wave of sentimental pity
> through their doubting hearts.

Donkin is a moral cadger, a robber of sentiment, an advance edition of the more subtle dereliction practiced by Wait, and he becomes the transmitter of Wait's metaphysical loafing. A fair-weather sailor, he is always the first to scream, to complain, to curse. "Venomous and thin-faced, he glared from the ample misfit of borrowed clothing as if looking for something he could smash." Alternately deriding and defending the Nigger, he is, appropriately enough, the only one present at his death, for it is fitting that Wait should vanish into darkness attended by his familiar spirit. Donkin discharges his futile hatred at the dying man, hurls a biscuit at him (the bread— the common bond) and steals his money (a subtle reversal of Single-ton at the pay table: Donkin finds *his* "small pile of gold in the pro-found darkness of" the deckhouse). In this death watch, Donkin suffers the terror of absolute moral isolation. And the animus of Wait inhabits the unholy frame of Donkin to the last. In his final appearance, at the Board of Trade pay-office, *dressed in another suit of clothes,* he pronounces maledictions on the assembled crew who have declined to drink with him:

"You won't drink? . . . No! . . . Then may ye die of thirst, every mother's son of yer! Not one of yer 'as the sperrit of a bug. Ye're the scum of the world. Work and starve!"

The mercurial Belfast suffers most, perhaps, from the burden of Wait's travesty of humility. Belfast is the man who steals the pie for Jimmy, who pulls him head-long from the deckhouse, who per-suades the poised corpse to leave the ship. His oversentient imagina-tion springs from love unconditioned by clear discrimination of its object and he remains in hysterical subjection to a Beelzebub whom he has mistaken for a divinity. On shore he begs piteously for a relic of Wait's belongings which have been sealed up and delivered to the Board of Trade. Through his inconsolable affection for the departed he articulates, incompletely, the character of Wait as scapegoat:

"You were his chum, too . . . but I pulled him out . . . didn't I? Short wool he had . . . He wouldn't go . . . He wouldn't go for no-body!" He burst into tears. "I never touched him—never—never!" he sobbed. "He went, for me, like . . . like . . . a lamb."

V

The iconography of *The Nigger of the "Narcissus"* was not ac-complished without a dangerous compromise between the naturalistic,

biographical material and its symbolic transmutation, as I have foot-
noted above. Fearful of overstressing the subaqueous world of the
underconsciousness, the symbol-producing level of the psyche which,
in fact, was the most dependable source of his inspiration, Conrad
overloaded his mundane treatment of the crew. As separate units
of consciousness they are beautifully deployed for angles of relationship, but no one can deny that their professional virtues are over-
written, almost to the detriment of the narrative's aesthetic integrity.
It is clear, in this direction, that Conrad had difficulty in serving myth
and memory with equal justice. His narrator-perspective is awkwardly
handled. The novel gets under way in the third person; in the middle
of the second chapter it switches abruptly to the viewpoint of first
person plural and remains there until the coda section, when it becomes first person singular. Presumably an unspecified member of the
deck crew has carried the narration; in this case the contents of the
thoughts of Mr. Creighton and of the cook, and many of the conversations, between Allistoun and his officer or between Donkin and Wait,
for example, are impossibly come by. And, with this handicap, the
gilded sermonizings on the crew's high endeavor are doubly hard to
accept. If Conrad was solicitous for the phenomenal level of his narrative, he might at least have supplied a recorder to whose endowments
his own opulent prose would have been more apt. However, this novel
was an early trial in the marriage of subject with its coordinating
agencies; Conrad's craft was not yet wholly adequate to sustain an un-
failing integrity of means.

Most curiously, quite apart from stylistic considerations, the novel
prefigures the inhibition that Conrad thereafter suffered from in developing or acknowledging his more clairvoyant perceptions. Neither
in the famous preface, appended to the 1914 edition, and the foreword that accompanied it, nor in his private communications on the
subject, will one find any admission of cabalistic intent. The aesthetic
of the preface, with its eloquent impressionism, is far too general to
have any more bearing on this novel than on any other. The foreword guards the secret skillfully, while teasing suspicion that there is a
secret: ". . . in the book he [Wait] is nothing; he is merely the center
of the ship's collective psychology and the pivot of the action." Merely!
Overt suggestions that he had enlisted transpersonal powers always
launched Conrad into protests of respectability and of allegiance to
the terrestrial, into panicky and often absurd interpretations of his
own work (witness his fantastic explanations of "The Secret Sharer"
and of *The Shadow Line*), into willful distortion of some of his finest

literary efforts. But D. H. Lawrence has warned us: "Never trust the artist. Trust the tale."

The Nigger of the "Narcissus" is a fable with many layers of interconnection. "A work that aspires, however humbly, to the condition of art, should carry its justification in every line." So begins the preface to this work and insofar as the novel, itself, seeks to establish "the power of occult forces which," Conrad concedes elsewhere, "rule the fascinating aspects of the visible world," it does carry its justification. Without the other dimensions, it would be merely a tale of ships and men burdened by an iridescent futility of expression. As it is, the metaphors which significantly cluster at every magnetic point in the narrative illuminate the infernal core of its theme as, on the equator, the *Narcissus* floats in the aurora of the lightning, "like a charred ship enclosed in a globe of fire."

Jimmy Wait and the Dance of Death:

Conrad's *Nigger of the "Narcissus"*

by Cecil Scrimgeour

> Knowledge takes up no position, sets no store by form. It has compassion within the abyss—it *is* the abyss. So we reject it, firmly, and henceforth our concern shall be with beauty only.
>
> > (G. Aschenbach, quoting Socrates' words to Phaedrus, in Thomas Mann's *Death in Venice*.)

I

When Joseph Conrad completed *The Nigger of the "Narcissus"* in January 1897, he was just emerging from his novitiate as a writer. The story had cost him great travail of spirit. While he worked at it, his mood had been that of a man fighting the trolls within himself and conducting a judgement session upon himself. As deeply as his Norwegian contemporary Ibsen, he had felt the need to use his art to get right with himself morally. Through scenes from the seafaring life, shaped partly from memories and partly out of visionary imagination, he had found means of dominating the fears that rose obsessively within him.

In the Preface to the story he alludes to this descent within himself, "in that lonely region of stress and strife" which had become for him the artist's own home ground. Having found the struggle to understand himself so hard, he had no great hopes that he would in turn

"Jimmy Wait and the Dance of Death: Conrad's Nigger of the 'Narcissus,'" by Cecil Scrimgeour. From Critical Quarterly, *VII (Winter 1965), 339–52. © 1965 by Cecil Scrimgeour. Reprinted by permission of the author.*

be sympathetically understood by the public of the subscription libraries. Consequently, when in the subsequent months the story appeared serially and at last in book form, he was all the more grateful for the encouraging letters that were sent to him by the judicious few, among them Henry James. Nonetheless, the feeling of unrest, of "gnawing unbelief," that had played so great a part in creating the story and in fostering the attitude of fatalistic resignation with which he had let it go from him, did not leave him. To Cunninghame Graham he confided, half admitting the disturbing moral implications of the book:

> . . . I can quite see that, without thinking, they (i.e. the respectable folk) may feel an instinctive disgust. So be it. In my mind I picture the book as a stone falling in the water. It is gone and not a trace shall remain. (Letter of Dec. 14, 1897.)

In other letters written to this correspondent about the same time Conrad unburdened himself about the discomfort of spirit he had been enduring. It sprang, in effect, from a common contemporary condition—from a subversion of belief, from doubt about the purposefulness of the world of nature and about the place of man, moral man, within it. Conrad's problem was the problem of a whole generation of writers, that of Hardy and Butler and Shaw. On the one hand, the world-picture offered by the doctrine of evolution presented nature as morally neutral, as a mechanism that, despite men's prayers, runs automatically on.

> There is a—let us say—machine. It evolved itself (I am severely scientific) out of a chaos of scraps of iron and behold!—it knits. I am horrified at the horrible work and stand appalled. I feel it ought to embroider —but it goes on knitting. . . . And the most withering thought is that the infamous thing has made itself: made itself without thought, without conscience, without foresight, without eyes, without heart. It is a tragic accident—and it has happened. You can't interfere with it. . . . It knits us in and it knits us out. It has knitted time, space, pain, death, corruption, despair and all the illusions—and nothing matters. (Letter to R. B. Cunninghame Graham, Dec. 20, 1897.)

Nor could Conrad, when he turned to the other half in the universal cleavage, to man with his mind and feelings, find any grounds for consolatory hope. About Conrad there is certainly none of that hopefulness that had sustained the sceptic T. H. Huxley when, three years earlier, he had delivered his Romanes Lecture (i.e. "Evolution and Ethics"). There Huxley, accepting the contradiction within the universe, had developed his vision of man using his moral strength and creative energy to stake out for himself an ever larger and more secure encampment within the domain of recalcitrant nature.

Conrad would have liked to share this heroic view of man's power to master his circumstances. Indeed, he thought of ships as encroachments upon nature, challenging her indifference and her sovereignty over man. "A ship," he averred, "is a creature which we have brought into the world, as it were on purpose to keep us up to the mark." And, momentarily at least, he expressed, through the figures of the excellent Captains Allistoun and MacWhirr, an optimistic belief comparable with Huxley's that man could create aboard ship an enclave of virtue and discipline, and maintain it against the destructive assault of natural forces. As a permanent stance, however, Conrad found himself unable confidently to reassert the time-honoured values implicit in the seamen's code of devotion, or to subscribe to the more recent attempts to square moral man with a neutral universe. His own view was darkened by despair. When Mrs. Cunninghame Graham sent him a copy of *The Life of St. Teresa* which she had written, a work that revealed (as Conrad admitted) a world of mysticism wonderfully rich and suggestive, he returned thanks in a letter of extreme pessimism:

> What makes mankind tragic is not that they are the victims of nature, it is that they are conscious of it. To be part of the animal kingdom under the conditions of this earth is very well—but as soon as you know of your slavery, the pain, the anger, the strife—the tragedy begins. We can't return to nature, since we can't change our place in it. Our refuge is in stupidity, in drunkenness of all kinds, in lies, in beliefs, in murder, thieving, reforming, in negation, in contempt—each man according to the promptings of his particular devil. There is no morality, no knowledge, and no hope: there is only the consciousness of ourselves which drives us about a world that, whether seen in a convex or a concave mirror, is always but a vain and floating appearance. (Jan. 31, 1898.)

These letters, written while the world of *The Nigger of the "Narcissus"* was still much on Conrad's mind, afford us a useful gloss upon the story itself. Due allowance must naturally be made for the different kinds of apprehension that are involved and expressed in the rational discourse of the letters as compared with the imagined and dramatised particulars of the story. Nevertheless, the concerns that have sought outlet in the story lose none of their urgency for Conrad in the letters, and they are illuminating indeed on that account.

In *The Nigger of the "Narcissus,"* then, Conrad peers questioningly into the obscure, capricious life of nature, and also into those elements of human character which seem to their possessors to put them beyond the governance of nature and beyond her last argument, death. Nature and moral man, diversely presented, face one another as protagonists. In order to dramatise the moral issues that he is exploring Conrad invents a narrative in which two of the oldest and poetically most powerful myths are collapsed into unity: they are the Dance of Death and the Odyssey. The two themes are bound together by the Jonah-like figure of the negro seaman, James Wait. Before Conrad's brief saga can be complete, and the crew returned to its home port as safely as Odysseus to his Penelope, Jimmy has to settle his account with death, with "stalking death," his intimate. He dies within sight of the first land, the Island of Flores, and the crew are released by that event to exercise their seamanship quite single-mindedly and to bring their vessel to port. There they too have to come to the reckoning: at the payoff on Tower Hill, under the eyes of their captain, they have to endure an assessment of worth and work which is in fact more moral than financial.

II

The sea and death, nature in two of her most impenetrable mysteries, are the ultimate realities against which the crew of the *Narcissus* have to measure themselves. Both these forces, by reason of their very unpredictability, have the power, as the story reveals, to exalt men or to corrupt them. Conrad insists that a ship is but "a fragment detached from the earth"; life on board, because it is isolated from land entanglements and subject to certain simple but characteristic relationships between men, lends itself admirably to the artist's task —that of presenting man's endless struggle to gain a foothold for his honour and for civilised values upon nature's treacherous surface. We have quoted earlier Huxley's picture of man creating for himself an enclave of moral security and progress, his colony as it were upon nature's unfriendly territory. We may compare with this view the image with which Conrad chooses both to open and conclude his story—the image of the ship (when its master and crew behave with highest responsibility) as a pool of light created and maintained against the aggressive darkness:

> Mr. Baker, chief mate of the ship "Narcissus," stepped in one stride out of his lighted cabin into the darkness of the quarterdeck. (Opening words of Section I.)
> The roar of the town resembled the roar of topping breakers, merciless and strong, with a loud voice and cruel purpose; but overhead the

clouds broke; a flood of sunshine streamed down the walls of grimy houses. The dark knot of seamen drifted in sunshine. (Finale of Section V.)

These images of light severed from darkness accumulate throughout the story, and help to suggest quite subtly the differences of moral quality that exist among members of the crew. The standards by which they live are to be inferred from the decisiveness or the indecision with which individuals move across the frontier between this light and this darkness, and commit themselves to the realm on either side of it. Mr. Baker, that "model chief mate" who did not like "to part with a ship," moves from the light to the darkness with confidence, "in one stride," cleanly. On the other hand, there is an undertone of reserve about Conrad's description of the whole crew as they fade away on Tower Hill, in his last paragraph. He had already conceded them much admiration for the courage with which, when "tossing aloft, invisible in the night, they gave back yell for yell to a westerly gale." But, in his parting words, we feel that Conrad awards them a very uncertain moral status: they made a "dark knot," and they "drifted in sunshine." It is true that their unsteady gait arises from the convivial rounds they have stood one another in the public-houses; but it also arises, more deeply, from the doubts, still unresolved in Conrad's mind, whether this newer, less stable generation of seamen will be able to withstand the modern mammon of unrighteousness—that delusive power and glory towards which the stained, but momentarily sunlit face of the Mint now beckons them.

The circle of light outside Mr. Baker's cabin door is, then, a symbol of great importance, establishing the forestage, as it were, upon which the moral drama of the voyage is to be played out. Into that circle each seaman must step when he answers the roll call in Bombay harbour, the summons to responsible service of his ship. This ritual is presently subverted, when Jimmy the negro, the last aboard, makes his belated and dramatic appearance. He comes out of the unmastered, inhuman darkness; he belongs to it. With him, and with his hollow, metallic cough which seems reverberantly to have a life apart from his own—the first notes here of Conrad's countertheme, the *danse macabre*—with him it is the power of darkness that summons the crew and demands obedience. The being that till now has been "all a smudge" on the chief mate's list asserts itself. The negro's call: "Wait!" is not only a naming of himself, but also a claim to authority and attention. To fix every eye he looms like a Michelangelesque shape over everybody, his head "away up in the shadows of lifeboats," and his black face reflecting in its vigorous modelling the "deep shadows and shining lights" of a tortured personality, a face that is at once pitiable and repulsive. His presence evokes ambiguous emotions in Conrad's seaman narrator and among the crew. Later we are told that "a black mist emanated from him," killing all joy and laughter, and the narrator has difficulty in sorting out whether the rattling cough and the proud, tormented mask were those of Death's victim, or of Death itself.

> Was he a reality—or was he a sham—this ever-expected visitor of Jimmy's? We hesitated between pity and mistrust, while, on the slightest provocation, he shook before our eyes the bones of this bothersome and infamous skeleton. (Section II.)

This inscrutable figure lays the ship under his spell. While he is on board, it suffers the extremes of storm and doldrums. But, more insidiously, his presence unlooses a moral fever among the crew which runs to a climax of mutiny and even to murderous assault upon Captain Allistoun. He, poor uncomplicated man, stands angry and perplexed in the face of Jimmy's ascendancy. The fact is that, if the negro takes possession of the souls of his shipmates, the reason lies partly in a certain indeterminacy in their own natures that predisposes them to submit to him, and partly in Jimmy's outward shape which is so disturbing as to make the appearance and the reality of his case hard to separate.

III

Before Jimmy makes his entry upon the scene, Conrad treats us to a rehearsal of the kind of influence that the negro will wield, using this time the secondary figure, the Cockney seaman Donkin, as his protagonist of evil. In his own way Donkin is as repellent a creature as the negro, for he is a compound of artful dodger, sea lawyer, layabout and malice incarnate. Through him Conrad develops from the outset one of the main motives of the story. Donkin is, in an exaggerated way, representative of a new generation of seamen born into the conditions of late nineteenth-century urban and industrial civilisation. From those surroundings they have gathered habits of selfishness, moody introspection, and greed, and the corruption has penetrated so deeply that such members of the crew can give only an intermittent and imperfect loyalty to the ancient code by which the seaman vowed fidelity to captain and ship. Again, this new race of seamen, being children of the earth and of great cities, have become mentally and emotionally complex and restless. They have lost the power of drawing strength and health of spirit from putting to sea, for Conrad, like the poets of a long romantic tradition, was dedicated to the proposition that in embracing the sea and wrestling with its mystery men could undergo healthful purgation of spirit and learn to discover themselves. In Conrad's sea stories we find him many a time reaffirming Baudelaire's tragic rapture:

> Homme libre, toujours tu chériras la mer!
> La mer est ton miroir: tu contemples ton âme
> Dans le déroulement infini de sa lame,
> Et ton esprit n'est pas un gouffre moins amer.

The trouble with these latter-day seamen of the *Narcissus* is that when they face long and intimately the changing surface and unfathomable depths of the sea, they draw no joy from the encounter. They only become unsettled within themselves and uncertain of purpose. Not for them the contentment of which Conrad's narrator aboard the *Narcissus* writes with Old Testament piety:

> The true peace of God begins at any spot a thousand miles from the nearest land; and when He sends there the messengers of His might it is not in terrible wrath against crime, presumption and folly, but paternally, to chasten simple hearts—ignorant hearts that know nothing of life, and beat undisturbed by envy or greed. (Section II.)

By these simple standards of virtue and seamanship Donkin is scornfully and decisively rejected by Conrad; as decisively as that character feels himself accused and rejected by the silent sea and by the last light that flickers in Jimmy's eyes as he (Donkin) sneaks away with the dying negro's savings. Donkin gets "a bad discharge" at the payoff, which is the crew's judgement day, and he retires defiantly, to inhabit (as Conrad imagines) one of those affluent and shady circles that make up the landlubbers' inferno. In the eyes of the judge and paymaster, Captain Allistoun, the performance of the rest of the crew has fallen very far short also. During the storm they certainly showed tenacity and they would win praise from landsmen, but by his standards of nautical honour, their "best is no better than bad."

IV

Set over against the crew and its unstable elements, there stand, in Conrad's imaginative design, three figures who live by the principle of loyalty—Captain Allistoun, the chief mate Mr. Baker, and the ordinary seaman, Old Singleton. Their dedication to the ship is absolute, and in consequence their resentment of the seditious influence of Donkin and Wait goes deep. These three are men of uncomplex character, and each in his own way subscribes to a simple ethical code. Captain Allistoun, olympian in the fastness of the poop, judges men as he himself fears to be judged—by "an unforgiving God"; and it is a sufficient reminder of his role as God's deputy, ruling in this little world apart, that at the end he should sit "smiling thoughtfully at the cleared pay-table." He has played his part stoically, as though he were carrying the burden of a sinful inheritance and earning remission by the sweat of his brow. This remission shapes itself sentimentally, in his dream of ending his days deep in the country, "out of sight of the sea."

Sincere as is Conrad's admiration for the strength and the faith with which the captain matches his ship against the elements, it is upon Old Singleton that, in this area of the story's design, he lavishes a grander, a more epical imagination. Conrad's narrator shares the forecastle with him, and has only to turn his eyes sideways to behold this wonder, this patriarch among seamen.

> Alone in the dim emptiness of the sleeping forecastle he appeared bigger, colossal, very old; old as Father Time himself. . . . Yet he was only a child of time, a lonely relic of a devoured and forgotten generation. . . . The men who could understand his silence were gone— those men who knew how to exist beyond the pale of life and within sight of eternity. . . . They were the everlasting children of the mysterious sea. Their successors are the grown-up children of a discontented earth. . . . (Section I.)

So Conrad expends his lyricism upon him. The same spirit of mingled exultation and pity animates the magnificent pages in which Singleton, after thirty hours unbroken service at the helm during the storm, collapses in the forecastle. As he falls, he reaches for the short clay pipe which another old seaman takes from his mouth and silently proffers him. This gesture, perfectly imagined correlative that it is, realises more powerfully than any of the rhetorical effusions to which Conrad elsewhere resorts what the age-old ethic of the seamen, founded upon fidelity, claims of its adherents. Pitifully Singleton recognises the devastating truth that, for all his strength, an end will come soon enough to the figure that he, like all the others, has been treading in the dance of death. And the rhythm of that dance has been set by the pitiless, lurching sea.

Through Singleton Conrad takes us to the heart of the matter.

Long endurance on one of life's natural frontiers has made this aged seaman clairvoyant. He is the soothsayer of the ship. Among the crew only he is unmoved by Jimmy Wait's complaining and deathly cough. For Singleton dying is just another job to be done, and just as the job of sailing ships demands the exercise of all one's manhood, so the business of meeting death can be faced only with such strength as a man can call forth from his own solitary, responsible self. "Well, get on with your dying," he curtly tells the negro, "don't raise a blamed fuss with us over that job. We can't help you." With similar intuition the oracular Singleton senses that every man, either by his origin or by some compulsive code of honour, is fatally drawn to his own element—he, Singleton, to the sea where he will be buried, and Jimmy, that displaced child of the tropical forests, to the land, at first sight of which his dying spirit will depart.

V

To return now to the figure of mystery, with whom we started this study. What is the secret of Jimmy Wait's influence that, lying cossetted and inert in his cabin, he should for periods subvert all order on board and come near to mastering the ship? Apart from Singleton, who only once condescends a fascinated stare at the death's head in the negro's berth, none of the ship's company is untouched by his spell. The feelings that his presence calls forth run amuck in diverse forms in the individual seamen—extreme pity, extreme anger, extreme greed—and in their turn these symptoms of personal sickness become the cause of new disorder among the men collectively. Belfast, who is, incidentally, the only seaman whose devotion and pity for the negro outlasts the latter's death and puts to shame the egotistical emotionalism of his fellows in the forecastle, sets off a chain reaction of suspicions by stealing, in a spasm of sentimentality, the officers' fruit pie for the ailing negro. Again, the cook, who had lately proved his self-command by miraculously producing hot coffee in the heart of the storm, is moved by the sight of Jimmy wrestling with the shadows, and attempts the one feat that is dear to the salvationist. He will pluck the brand from the burning, and bring Jimmy to conviction of sin.

> Whenever I poke my galley fire I think of you chaps—swearing, stealing, lying, and worse. . . . Well, well. They will have a hot time of it. Hot! The furnaces of them White Star boats ain't nothing to it. (Section IV.)

The consequences of this incident, Jimmy's terror of hell fire, his admission of guilt as a malingerer, his solitary confinement, ultimately bring on mutiny and Donkin's boldest assertion of evil in assaulting the captain.

We have already commented upon the support that Jimmy and Donkin give one another in spreading moral unrest. We might add that in this relationship the mastery is really with the negro. Or is it with the negro's invisible associate, death? Donkin, despite his studied contempt for Jimmy, is drawn into his power by a consuming desire to race death for Jimmy's golden dollars. In this theft the insidious force that is released by the negro and his unseen partner takes its full triumph: under its sway Donkin destroys himself as a moral being. In the moment of success, with the dollars in hand, he achieves the final damnation that all his malice has been striving for. Death, leaning out of Jimmy's berth, touches him from behind, mocking his cunning:

> . . . at that moment he received the irresistible impression of something happening behind him. He spun round as though he had been tapped on the shoulder. He was just in time to see Wait's eyes blaze up and go out at once. . . . (Section V.)

Morally, too, Donkin is judged and cast out by all those (elements in nature and human persons alike) whose opinion, in Conrad's scheme of things, ultimately matters. We are told that he "slunk off noiselessly as if judged and cast out" by the sea; for all its "glittering surface and lightless depths" the "immortal sea" cannot be escaped as the supreme arbiter of a man's craftsmanship and honour. He is written off too by the captain who keeps men up to the test. And by his shipmates who, for all their wavering about moral issues, express an intuitive judgement of their fellows in the choice they make of those they drink with. By this last test Donkin, offering to treat them after the payoff, is left isolated and flat, a hollow man for all his affluent swagger and the dubious privilege of a good new job ashore.

In the character of Jimmy Wait Conrad creates one of those ambiguous figures in which contradictory worlds of feeling and moral value converge, a figure in which the complex inwardness of human experience is laid bare in paradox. Conrad's imagination imparts a subtle texture to the whole tale by exploring in much detail the dual attitude which the ordinary members of the crew take up towards the negro. For them Wait is both contemptible and pitiable, a work-shy unemployable and a sick man, a petty tyrant deserving of the same scorn as he himself deals out to his slaves. And yet at the same time he is a man of misfortunes to be solaced and cherished, nay, even courted, because easing his condition seems to promise some remedy that will ward off the calamities inflicted by the sea upon all of them. As the crew pass him from hand to hand in the teeth of the storm, after an heroic act of salvage, the narrator reflects:

> . . . Though at that time we hated him more than ever—more than anything under heaven—we did not want to lose him. We had so far saved him; and it had become a personal matter between us and the sea. (Section III.)

In this state of resentment against nature's capriciousness the crew is prepared to go to any lengths for Jimmy, the most lonely and most abject of her victims. They would even jeopardise their ship, and the craftsmanship upon which she sails, for his sake. The depth of this feeling, and the reckless extremes to which it drives them are perfectly rendered in the episode in which the carpenter's tools and nails, simple emblems of all the skills that hold a ship together, are hurled overboard in order to clear the way to the entombed negro. Because the issue is here so well enacted, we are compelled to feel the threat to standards of orderly seamanship that may arise from a well-intentioned and even laudable sentimentalism. This contradiction is once again brought to a dramatic point in a later incident. After the storm and the cook's assault on Jimmy's soul, the mood of the crew rises to a mutinous crescendo out of sympathy for him. The helmsman, of all men, abandons the wheel. The wind sharply reminds him of his dereliction of duty, and recalls the drifting ship to order.

> It was as if an invisible hand had given the ship an angry shake to recall the men that peopled her decks to the sense of reality, vigilance and duty.

At the climax of the mutiny the captain bluntly asks the crew: "Well, you see me now. What do you want?" The question comes from a man who, from training and experience, accepts the conditions of life, and meets them with a simple faith and a few orderly principles of behaviour. Those whom he challenges belong to another world and to a later generation. As we have seen, this generation is the product of an industrial and urban civilisation which, in Conrad's eyes, is satanic because it is held together by no stable ideals. Coming from such a background, these seamen are restless and rootless; the more sensitive of them, such as the narrator of the story (predecessor of Conrad's even more speculative explorer of men's characters and value, Marlow), are tossed this way and that, trying to make sense

out of contradiction and square the evolutionist's picture of nature's
mindless neutrality with the idea of progress. It may be that these
men in the *Narcissus* have taken to the sea because they feel themselves morally adrift, and a life divided between homeland and ship
answers their need. Their state resembles that of Baudelaire's deluded
seafarers:

> Mais les vrais voyageurs sont ceux-là seuls qui partent
> Pour partir; coeurs légers, semblables aux ballons.

The last memories that Conrad's narrator entertains of his former
shipmates are those of a body of men drifting "in sunlight," or drifting
by in the shadowy ship of death. So unsubstantial have they been,
and have they become. They take on a brief, insecure reality for him,
when there flashes back upon memory his last picture of them exer-
cising their manhood upon ship's tackle, fisting "the beating canvas
of a heavy foresail" in the storm.

The resentment of the crew against Captain Allistoun is, under
these circumstances, only the occasion for giving vent to a larger
rebellion:

> What did they want? Jimmy was forgotten; no one thought of him,
> alone forward in his cabin, fighting great shadows, clinging to brazen
> lies, chuckling painfully over his transparent deceptions. No, not Jimmy;
> he was forgotten more than if he had been dead. They wanted great
> things. And suddenly all the simple words they knew seemed to be lost
> for ever in the immensity of their vague and burning desire. (Section
> IV.)

In this slack, directionless condition—it is "the 'Melencolia' that
transcends all wit," described by the late Victorian poet James Thom-
son harking back to Dürer; it is Baudelaire's "ennui" in another
mode—the crew hover, unable to answer the claims that two opposed
principles of action press upon them. On the one hand, the ship and
its master exact an absolute loyalty and self-subordination; on the
other hand, they hear within their hearts the clamour for a vast personal freedom, the romantic and individualistic urges that are the
dominant motives of their century. The seafaring life, far from dull
urban entanglement, promises to satisfy these latter desires; yet they
are, in fact, rudely denied by the insecurity that lies within "the glittering surface and lightless depths" of the sea.

It is against that fatal insecurity, against the limiting conditions of
life, that Jimmy's courtiers are protesting when they haunt his cabin
and enact an absurd charade of lying and flattery for his benefit. It is
not easy for the narrator to decide who or what it is they are seeking

to charm and placate: is it the dying negro or death whose shape he assumes?

> He was becoming immaterial like an apparition; his cheekbones rose, the forehead slanted more; the face was all hollows, patches of shade; and the fleshless head resembled a disinterred black skull, fitted with two restless globes of silver in the sockets of eyes. (Section V.)

As they minister to Jimmy, the crew plunge into ever deeper dishonesty and self-deception. From the tone of the writing we can sense the great artistic enjoyment that Conrad derives from discriminating between the subtle moral ambiguities that overtake the crew in this attempt to beguile Jimmy and cheat Death. They will "keep Jimmy alive till home"; they will annul the siege of Death by pretending what is manifestly false—that he is not there. The deceptions are so gross, and in so good a cause, that the corruption that they engender in each man's heart easily invades the whole person. Conrad strains all the refinements of verb, noun, and epithet to analyse the equivocations into which the crew in its dilemma falls:

> He (Jimmy) was demoralising. Through him we were becoming highly humanised, tender, complex, excessively decadent: we understood the subtlety of his fear, sympathised with all his repulsions, shrinking, evasions, delusions—as though we had been overcivilised, and rotten, and without any knowledge of the meaning of life. (Section V.)

The cleavage in the narrator's mind, between admiration for the ancient and imperative seaman's code of honour and sympathy for the new man's rebellious protest, reflects a similar cleavage within Conrad himself. He gives it symbolic shape in the paradox of the crew's false fidelity to Jimmy. More than that, Conrad allows the dialectical argument within himself to play itself out in the conflict between the central figures, Captain Allistoun and the negro. This struggle for mastery between them is eventually resolved by the interposition of a power greater than both of them.

Death must have her way with Jimmy, and—what is perhaps more important—be accepted as the final reality by the crew, before they are all purged of their moral sickness and before the reawakening winds can carry them home. In another way, the very ship *Narcissus* itself has to endure and accept death before her men can come before the master at the payoff table and receive judgement on their handling of sail and helm. To complete her mission the ship must suffer the embrace of the alien earth, and the earth has already, in the manner of Jimmy's dying, been correlated with death.

The "Narcissus" came gently into her berth; the shadows of soulless walls fell upon her, the dust of all the continents leaped upon her deck, and a swarm of strange men, clambering up her sides, took possession of her in the name of the sordid earth. She had ceased to live. (Section V.)

In this world of pitiless nature and human illusions acceptance of death is the first step towards liberation and health of spirit. When Belfast cries to Jimmy's corpse that seems so reluctant to slip down the board into the sea: "Be a man! . . . Go, Jimmy, go" he voices the crew's desire to be relieved for good of their burden and responsibility; but he also expresses what they all know in their hearts. They now know that the meaning of life is to be found in the way a man asserts his own manhood, and that he is released to take possession of himself most completely when he ceases evading the reality of death and accepts it. Because the crew of the *Narcissus*, after their fever of self-indulgence and fear, have come to act upon this truth, and found momentary strength from it, Conrad's narrator, in his last elegiac salute to them, gives them all an affectionate indulgence:

. . . On the waters of the forlorn stream drifts a ship—a shadowy ship manned by a crew of Shades. They pass and make a sign, in a shadowy hail. Haven't we, together and upon the immortal sea, wrung a meaning from our sinful lives? Good-bye, brothers! You were a good crowd. (Section V.)

For Conrad, then, moral courage, a stoic firmness in facing evil and dissolution, was the highest good that man can wrest from life. In this respect there is in this story an interesting anticipation, perhaps a rehearsal, of a situation that was shortly, and with maturer art, to engage Conrad's imagination. In *The Heart of Darkness* the narrator Marlow relates a train of adventures in which he tracks down in the Congo forest the rascally ivory-trader, Mr. Kurtz. Marlow reflects upon the moral implications of the man's life, and especially upon the manner of his dying. At the moment of death Mr. Kurtz had sat up and cried: "The horror!" To Marlow it seems, in retrospect, that there had been, despite appearances, a certain moral strength about the old trader. He had taken a straight look at all the evil in his own nature, and his cry had represented his recoil before the abyss into which he had sunk. Against all expectations this degraded man had reasserted his human dignity in passing so strict a final judgement on the state of his own soul.

The situation of Mr. Kurtz is prefigured in the impressions that Captain Allistoun confides to his chief mate after the evangelising

cook has struck terror into Jimmy Wait. The captain catches sight of
the same horrible abyss reflected in Jimmy's eyes:

> Did you see the eyes of that sick nigger, Mr. Baker? I fancy he begged
> me for something. What? Past all help. One lone black beggar amongst
> the lot of us, and he seemed to look through me into the very hell. . . .
> Well, let him die in peace. I am master here after all. Let him be. He
> might have been half a man once. . . . (Section IV.)

The scene of Jimmy's "looking into the very hell" is later enacted in
strict actuality under the eyes of the thieving Donkin. Not here,
however, do we have the feeling, as with Mr. Kurtz, of a man moving,
in one act of self-judgement, into a fuller dimension of moral nature.
Jimmy's words, sobbed out with "an incredibly strong and heart-
breaking voice" as he faces his own seaman's burial and the onset of
"unspeakable horrors," are: "Overboard! . . . I! . . . My God!" It
is the individualist's and the romantic's protest against the extinction
of consciousness—that consciousness which assures man of having a
certain, but brief superiority over the destructiveness of delusive nature and her ally, death. The prospect of dying opens out no new
adventure to Conrad's character; it offers none of the mystical hopefulness that had earlier in the century raised the spirit of Baudelaire's
disillusioned traveller:

> O Mort! vieux capitaine, il est temps! levons l'ancre!
> Ce pays nous ennuie, o Mort! Appareillons! . . .
> Nous voulons, tant ce feu nous brûle le cerveau,
> Plonger au fond du gouffre, Enfer ou Ciel, qu'importe?
> Au fond de l'Inconnu pour trouver du *nouveau*!

On the contrary, for Conrad (he speaks through the narrator) "a gone
shipmate, like any other man, is gone for ever."

Those who sail in ships, hoping narcissistically to discover the true
image of their moral selves thrown back by the sea, will find, Conrad
suggests, only disillusion. Although seafaring may provide the conditions under which a man may prove and find himself, he will not,
in effect, draw life-giving strength from the elements themselves. To
Jimmy and to the narrator the face of nature gives back an image
of indestructible energy and annihilating cruelty, masked momentarily
by displays of unbelievable beauty and peace.

> Life seemed (i.e. to Jimmy lying in the becalmed ship) an indestruct-
> ible thing. It went on in darkness, in sunshine, in sleep; tireless, it hov-
> ered affectionately round the imposture of his ready death. It was bright,
> like the twisted flare of lightning, and more full of surprises than the

dark night. It made him safe, and the calm of its overpowering darkness was as precious as its restless and dangerous light. (Section IV.)

In the magnificence of the phantom rays the ship appeared pure like a vision of ideal beauty, illusive like a tender dream of serene peace. And nothing in her was real, nothing was distinct and solid but the heavy shadows that filled her decks with their unceasing and noiseless stir: the shadows darker than the night and more restless than the thoughts of men.

Donkin prowled spiteful and alone amongst the shadows, thinking that Jimmy too long delayed to die. . . . (Section V.)

In these descriptions, however, we are made to feel that the solace of such moments is quite unreal, and that, like the heavy, unstable shadows which play about the negro and in which Donkin skulks, "all is in an enormous dark drowned."

I began this study of the *Nigger of the "Narcissus"* by pointing out that Conrad had couched his story in the form of a Dance of Death. It is a handling of the traditional theme made unusually complex by the infusion of late nineteenth-century pessimism. So subtle are the invading doubts that Conrad finds it hard to keep his balance. A dance, in effect, presupposes design:

> Except for the point, the still point,
> There would be no dance, and there is only the dance.

The still points of Conrad's design are the characters of simple men, Allistoun, Baker, Singleton, who hold their world together by the strength that they draw from within themselves. The dignity that attends them springs not merely from their skill as craftsmen, but also from their ability to endure situations of extreme moral stress without taking refuge in sentimentality or seeking relief in malice.

The Nigger of the "Narcissus"

by Albert J. Guerard

The complexities of *Almayer's Folly* are those of a man learning—
and with what a perverse instinct for the hardest way!—the language
of the novelist. *The Nigger of the "Narcissus"* is the first of the books
to carry deliberately and with care the burden of several major interests and various minor ones. The one interest which existed for most
readers in 1897 remains a real one today: the faithful document of
life and adventure at sea. The story is indeed the tribute to the
"children of the sea" that Conrad wanted it to be: a memorial to a
masculine society and the successful seizing of a "passing phase of
life from the remorseless rush of time."[1] It is certainly a tribute to
this particular ship on which (for her beauty) Conrad chose to sail
in 1884. But it is also a study in collective psychology; and also,
frankly, a symbolic comment on man's nature and destiny; and also,
less openly, a prose-poem carrying overtones of myth. No small burden, and one which Conrad carried with more care than usual: one
passage exists in as many as seven versions.[2] "It is the book by which,
not as a novelist perhaps, but as an artist striving for the utmost
sincerity of expression, I am willing to stand or fall."[3]

A rich personal novel can hardly be overinterpreted, but it can be
misinterpreted easily enough. The dangers of imbalance are suggested
by three other masculine narratives which similarly combine faithful
reporting and large symbolic suggestion. *The Red Badge of Courage*
may well present a sacramental vision and still another of the ubiq-

---

"The Nigger of the 'Narcissus.'" *Reprinted by permission of the publishers from
Albert J. Guerard,* Conrad the Novelist (*Cambridge, Mass.: Harvard University
Press, 1958*), *pp. 100–14.* © *1958 by the President and Fellows of Harvard College.*

[1] Preface, *The Nigger of the "Narcissus."*

[2] John D. Gordan, *Joseph Conrad: The Making of a Novelist* (Cambridge, Mass.,
1941), pp. 141–44.

[3] "To My Readers in America" (Preface of 1914), *The Nigger of the "Narcissus."*

uitous Christ figures which bemuse criticism; the patterns of imagery
are challenging. But it is also, importantly, a record of military life.
So too I would allow that "The Bear" contains primitive pageant-
rites, initiation ritual, the Jungian descent into the unconscious, perhaps even the Jungian mandala. These matters put the critic on his
mettle. But he should acknowledge that some of the story's best pages
concern hunting in the big woods and the vanishing of these woods
before commercial encroachment. The dangers of imbalance are even
more serious when provoked by a slighter work, such as *The Old Man
and the Sea*. To say that the novel is about growing old, or about the
aging artist's need to substitute skill for strength, is plausible. But
can a critic be satisfied with so little? One has gone so far as to find
a parable of the decline of the British Empire. This, I submit, takes
us too far from the boat and the marlin attached to its side; from the
small greatness of a story whose first strength lies in its faithful record-
ing of sensations, of fishing and the sea.

The Nigger of the "Narcissus" (sixty years after the event) is pecul-
iarly beset with dangers for the critic. For Conrad has become fashionable rather suddenly, and comment on this story has passed almost
without pause from naive recapitulation to highly sophisticated analysis of "cabalistic intent." The older innocence is suggested by Arthur
Symons' complaint that the story had no idea behind it, or by a
journeyman reviewer's remark that James Wait had no place in this
record of life at sea.[4] An example of recent sophistication is Vernon
Young's important essay "Trial by Water," in the Spring 1952 issue
of *Accent*. A single sentence will suggest its bias: "Fearful of overstressing the subaqueous world of the underconsciousness, the symbol-
producing level of the psyche which, in fact, was the most dependable
source of his inspiration, Conrad overloaded his mundane treatment
of the crew." The comment is provocative; it leads us to wonder
whether the crew isn't, for this fiction, too numerous. Yet we must
rejoin that the crew is very important, and that many of the book's
greatest pages have little to do with this subaqueous world. There
remains the vulgar charge yet real menace that the critic may over-
simplify a novel by oversubtilizing and overintellectualizing it—not
merely by intruding beyond the author's conscious intention (which
he is fully privileged to do) but by suggesting patterns of unconscious
combination which do not *and cannot operate* for the reasonably alert
common reader. Much of any serious story works on the fringes of the
reader's consciousness: a darkness to be illumined by the critic's in-

---

[4] Gordan, *Joseph Conrad*, pp. 289, 286.

sight. But that insight remains irrelevant which can never become aesthetic enjoyment, or which takes a story too far out of its own area of discourse. I say this with the uneasy conviction that criticism should expose itself to as many as possible of a novel's suasions, and that it is only too easy (above all with a Conrad or a Faulkner) to stress the abstract and symbolic at the expense of everything else. One might begin by saying that *The Nigger of the "Narcissus"* recasts the story of Jonah and anticipates "The Secret Sharer" 's drama of identification. This is a truth but a partial truth. And how many partial truths would be needed to render or even evoke such a mobile as this one. Touch one wire, merely breathe on the lovely thing and it wavers to a new form! In the pursuit of structured meaning—of obvious purpose and overtone of conviction and "cabalistic intent" and unconscious content; of stark symbol and subtle cluster of metaphor—one is tempted to ignore the obvious essentials of technique and style. One may even never get around to mentioning what are, irrespective of structure or concealed meaning, the best-written pages in the book. They are these: the arrival of James Wait on board, the onset of the storm, the overturning of the ship, the righting of the ship, old Singleton at the wheel, the quelling of the mutiny, the death of Wait and his burial, the docking of the ship, the dispersal of the crew.

It seems proper for once to begin with the end: with that large personal impression which an embarrassed criticism often omits altogether. *The Nigger of the "Narcissus"* is the most generalized of Conrad's novels in its cutting of a cross-section, though one of the least comprehensive. It is a version of our dark human pilgrimage, a vision of disaster illumined by grace. The microcosmic ship is defined early in the second chapter with an almost Victorian obviousness: "On her lived truth and audacious lies; and, like the earth, she was unconscious, fair to see—and condemned by men to an ignoble fate. The august loneliness of her path lent dignity to the sordid inspiration of her pilgrimage. She drove foaming to the south as if guided by the courage of a high endeavour." Or we can narrow the vision to a single sentence near the end: "The dark knot of seamen drifted in sunshine." The interplay of light and dark images throughout conveys the sense of a destiny both good and evil, heroic and foolish, blundered out under a soulless sky. If I were further to reduce the novel to a single key-word, as some critics like to do, I should choose the word *grace*. In thematic terms not the sea but life at sea is pure and life on earth sordid. Yet the pessimism of *The Nigger of the "Narcissus"* is (unlike that of *The Secret Agent*) a modified pessimism, and the gift of grace can circumvent thematic terms. Thus England herself is once imaged as a great ship. The convention of the novel is that the gift of grace may fall anywhere, or anywhere except on the Donkins. The story really ends with the men clinging for a last moment to their solidarity and standing near the Mint, that most representative object of the sordid earth:

> The sunshine of heaven fell like a gift of grace on the mud of the earth, on the remembering and mute stones, on greed, selfishness; on the anxious faces of forgetful men. And to the right of the dark group the stained front of the Mint, cleansed by the flood of light, stood out for a moment dazzling and white like a marble palace in a fairy tale. The crew of the *Narcissus* drifted out of sight.[5]

So the novel's vision is one of man's dignity but also of his "irremediable littleness"—a conclusion reached, to be sure, by most great works in the Christian tradition. In "Heart of Darkness," *Lord Jim*, and "The Secret Sharer" we have the initiatory or expiatory descents within the self of individual and almost lost souls; in *Nostromo* we shall see the vast proliferation of good and evil in history and political institution. But *The Nigger of the "Narcissus"* presents the classic human contradiction (and the archetypal descent into self) in collective terms, reduced to the simplicities of shipboard life. The storm tests and brings out the solidarity, courage, and endurance of men banded together in a desperate cause. And the Negro James Wait tests and brings out their egoism, solitude, laziness, anarchy, fear. The structural obligation of the story is to see to it that the two tests do not, for the reader, cancel out.

Presented so schematically, Conrad's vision may seem truly Christian. But this is indeed a soulless sky. In the restless life of symbols sunlight is converted, at one point, to that in human Nature which Man must oppose. The Norwegian sailor who chatters at the sun has lost his saving separateness from Nature, and when the sun sets his voice goes out "together with the light." The "completed wisdom" of old Singleton (one of the first Conrad extroverts to achieve some of his own skepticism) sees "an immensity tormented and blind, moaning and furious. . . ." And in one of the novel's central intellectual statements (the first paragraph of the fourth chapter) the indifferent sea is metaphorically equated with God, and the gift of grace is defined as labor, which prevents man from meditating "at ease upon the complicated and acrid savour of existence." The dignity of man lies in his vast silence and endurance: a dignity tainted by those who

---

[5] *The Nigger of the "Narcissus,"* p. 172.

clamor for the reward of another life. The message is rather like
Faulkner's, and these good seamen are like "good Negroes." But here
too, as in other novels of Conrad, man's works and institutions must
prepare him to profit from even such grace as this. From our human
weakness and from the eternal indifference of things we may yet be
saved . . . by authority, tradition, obedience. Thus the only true
grace is purely human and even traditional. There are certain men
(specifically Donkin) who remain untouched. But such men exist
outside: outside our moral universe which is both dark and light but
not inextricably both. And James Wait, as sailor and person rather
than symbol? I am not sure. He seems to suffer from that "empti-
ness" which would be Kurtz's ruin: "only a cold black skin loosely
stuffed with soft cotton wool . . . a doll that had lost half its sawdust."

This, speaking neither in terms of gross obvious intentions and
themes nor of unconscious symbolic content but of generalized human
meaning and ethical bias, is what *The Nigger of the "Narcissus"* says.
This is its reading of life.

"My task which I am trying to achieve is, by the power of the
written word to make you hear, to make you feel—it is, before all,
to make you *see*." [6] The sea story is beyond praise; there is no need
to defend the amount of space and emphasis Conrad gives it. The
long third chapter on the storm is one of the summits of Conrad, and
the pages on the righting of the ship one of the summits of English
prose. This is, as few others, a real ship. At the start the solidarity of
the forecastle is built up gradually, presumably as on any ship, then
disrupted by the foul Donkin and the lazy, narcissistic Wait. A sham
fellowship first occurs when the seamen give clothing to Donkin, and
is increased by their lazy sympathy for the malingering Negro. The
true solidarity is created by the exigencies of the storm, and during
the worst hours of crisis the good seamen are significantly separated
from Wait, who is trapped in his cabin, buried. With the storm over
the individuals again become Individuals, and by the same token
capable of mutiny. In the Conrad universe we often have this sense
of a few men banded together in desperate opposition to a cosmic
indifference and to human nature itself. For this voyage ordinary men
have come together, been isolated by their weaknesses, and have come
together again. On land they separate once more; for one last poignant

⁶ Preface, *The Nigger of the "Narcissus."*

moment they are the dark knot of seamen drifting in sunshine. "Good-bye brothers! You were a good crowd. As good a crowd as ever fisted with wild cries the beating canvas of a heavy foresail; or tossing aloft, invisible in the night, gave back yell for yell to a westerly gale." The novel is also about that solidarity Conrad admired but rarely drama-tized.

In these last sentences of the novel Conrad himself is speaking, rather than the anonymous narrator. And this is perhaps the best place to consider the often noted waywardness in point of view. The novel opens with objective reporting, and the first narrative voice we hear is stiff, impersonal, detached, a voice reading stage directions. But Conrad's natural impulse is to write in the first person, if possible retrospectively; to suggest action and summarize large segments of time. His natural impulse is to meditative and often ironic with-drawal. (It is author not narrator who pauses to comment on the popularity of Bulwer-Lytton among seamen: an extreme withdrawal.) On the seventh page the narrator momentarily becomes a member of the crew, but we must wait until the second chapter for this identifica-tion to be made frankly. Meanwhile we may detect in Conrad a restless impatience with the nominal objectivity adopted—a coolness of man-ner sharply broken through as he speaks out his admiration for Single-ton, his contempt for Donkin. Passionate conviction energized Con-rad's visualizing power as nothing else in the chapter did; and we have immortally the Donkin of white eyelashes and red eyelids, with "rare hairs" about the jaws, and shoulders "peaked and drooped like the broken wings of a bird. . . ."

With the second chapter, and the sailing of the ship, the prose takes on poetic qualities. A meditative observer outside and above the *Narcissus* sees her as "a high and lonely pyramid, gliding, all shining and white, through the sunlit mist." We return briefly to the deck for a paragraph of flat reporting, then have the developed and Vic-torian analogy of the ship and the earth with its human freight. The paragraph has the kind of obviousness an intentionalist would wel-come, but I suspect its real purpose was tactical. By generalizing his ship in this gross fashion, Conrad freed himself from the present moment and from the obligation to report consecutively. "The days raced after one another, brilliant and quick like the flashes of a light-house, and the nights, eventful and short, resembled fleeting dreams." And now he can pursue his natural mode: to hover selectively over a large segment of time, dipping down for a closer view only when he chooses. On the next page (as though to achieve still further

retrospective freedom) the narrator identifies himself as a member
of the crew. Suddenly we are told that Mr. Baker "kept all our noses
to the grindstone."

The subsequent waverings of point of view are the ones that have
disturbed logicians. Vernon Young puts their case clearly: "Presumably an unspecified member of the deck crew has carried the narration; in this case the contents of the thoughts of Mr. Creighton and
of the cook, and many of the conversations, between Allistoun and
his officer or between Donkin and Wait, for example, are impossibly
come by." [7] The classic answer to such logic is that all eggs come from
the same basket. It may be given more lucidly thus: the best narrative
technique is the one which, however imperfect logically, enlists the
author's creative energies and fully explores his subject. We need only
demand that the changes in point of view not violate the reader's
larger sustained vision of the dramatized experience. Creighton's
thoughts (since he is no more nor less than a deck officer) can violate
nothing except logic. But serious violation does occur twice: when we
are given Wait's broken interior monologues (pages 113, 149). For
we are approaching the mysterious Negro's death, and it has been the
very convention of the novel that Wait must remain shadowy, vast,
provocative of large speculation; in a word, symbolic. The very fact
that he comes in some sense to represent our human "blackness"
should exempt him from the banalities of everyday interior monologue. It would be as shocking to overhear such interior monologue
of Melville's Babo or of Leggatt in "The Secret Sharer."

For the rest, the changes in point of view are made unobtrusively
and with pleasing insouciance. What is more deadly than the ratio-
cinations of a narrator trying to explain his "authority," as the Marlow
of *Chance* does? The movement of point of view through this novel
admirably reflects the general movement from isolation to solidarity to
poignant separation. So the detached observer of the first pages becomes an anonymous member of the crew using the word "we." He
works with the others during the storm and joins them in the rescue
of Wait; and he too, both actor and moralizing spectator, becomes
prey to sentimentalism, laziness, fear. Then in the final pages the
"we" become an "I," still a nameless member of the crew but about
to become the historical Joseph Conrad who speaks in the last paragraph. "I disengaged myself gently." The act of meditative with-
drawal at last becomes complete. Approach and withdrawal, the ebb

---

[7] Vernon Young, "Trial by Water," *Accent* (Spring 1952), pp. 80–81. [See pp. 25–
39 of this volume.]

and flow of a generalizing imagination which cannot leave mere primary experience alone—these are, in any event, the incorrigible necessities of the early Conrad, and they account for some of his loveliest effects.

So we have first of all, reported and meditated, the sea story and memorial realism suggested by the early American title, *The Children of the Sea*. But there is also (and almost from the beginning) the insufferable Negro James Wait. In his own right he is mildly interesting: as a lonely and proud man who is about to die, as an habitual malingerer whose canny deception becomes at last desperate self-deception. But his role in the novel is to provide the second test; or, as Conrad puts it in his American preface, "he is merely the centre of the ship's collective psychology and the pivot of the action." Merely! His role is to provoke that sympathetic identification which is the central chapter of Conrad's psychology, and through it to demonstrate Conrad's conviction that sentimental pity is a form of egoism. In their hidden laziness the members of the crew sympathize with Wait's malingering; later, seeing him die before their eyes, they identify their own chances of survival with his. The process of identification (dramatized with little explanation in *Lord Jim*) is defined explicitly here:

> Falsehood triumphed. It triumphed through doubt, through stupidity, through pity, through sentimentalism. . . . *The latent egoism of tenderness to suffering appeared in the developing anxiety not to see him die.* . . . He was demoralising. Through him we were becoming highly humanised, tender, complex, excessively decadent: we understood the subtlety of his fear, sympathized with all his repulsions, shrinkings, evasions, delusions—as though we had been over-civilised, and rotten, and without any knowledge of the meaning of life.[8]

It could be argued that Conrad recapitulates too obviously, and reiterates rather too often, Wait's demoralizing influence. But the process of irrational identification was little understood by readers in 1897, or in fact by many readers since. It required explication. Thus the sentence I have italicized, almost the central statement of the novel, was omitted in Robert d'Humières' translation.[9] The "egoism of tenderness to suffering" must have struck him as meaningless.

Such, on the "mundane" or naturalistic level of psychology, is the function of Wait; and even the captain is finally corrupted by pity.

---

[8] *The Nigger of the "Narcissus,"* pp. 138, 139.
[9] This was called to my attention by Mrs. Elizabeth Von Klemperer, who is preparing a dissertation on James and Conrad in France.

He pretends to share in Wait's self-deception: "Sorry for him—like you would be for a sick brute. . . . I thought I would let him go out in his own way. Kind of impulse." And this moment of pity causes the incipient mutiny. As for the crew, they cared nothing for Wait as a human being, hated him in fact, but had accepted him as a precious token. "We wanted to keep him alive till home—to the end of the voyage." But this is, of course, impossible. James Wait must die in sight of land, as Singleton said, and the *Narcissus* cannot finish her voyage until the body of Wait (like the living bodies of Leggatt and of Jonah) has been deposited into the sea. Then but only then the "ship rolled as if relieved of an unfair burden; the sails flapped." And the ship rushes north before a freshening gale. To the personal and psychological-naturalistic burden of Wait is added—almost "unfairly" for a story of little more than 50,000 words—the burden of an audacious symbolic pattern. In certain early pages Wait is A Death, and a test of responses to death. But ultimately he is written in larger terms: *as something the ship and the men must be rid of before they can complete their voyage.* What this something is—more specific than a "blackness"—is likely to vary with each new reader. But its presence as part of the wavering mobile, as a force the story must allow for, raises crucial questions of technique.

Conrad's task, briefly, was to respect both flesh ("A negro in a British forecastle is a lonely being")[10] and symbol; to convey a vivid black human presence which could yet take on the largest meanings; which could become, as in Melville, "the Negro." Conrad faces the double challenge with the moment Wait steps on board, calling out that name which is mistaken for an impertinent command, "Wait!" Whether or not Vernon Young is right in detecting a play on the word (Wait: weight, burden), symbolic potentialities exist from the start. As we shall first see of Leggatt only a headless corpse floating in the water, so here we see only a body. "His head was away up in the shadows." And—cool, towering, superb—the Nigger speaks the words which, in a true morality, a symbolic force might speak: "I belong to the ship." But what saves the scene (what prevents the reader from detecting larger meanings too soon) is its concrete reality. The ambiguous arrival at once provokes action and talk, a dramatic interchange. And when it is over the magnitude of the Nigger is firmly established. We are able to accept that first "cough metallic, hollow, and tremendously loud," resounding "like two explosions in a vault."

I would insist, in other words, that Old Ben is also a real bear,

---

[10] "To My Readers in America."

and Babo a fleshly slave, and Moby Dick a real whale, and James Wait (though his name was "all a smudge" on the ship's list) a proud consumptive Negro. It is truly the critic's function to suggest potentialities and even whole areas of discourse that a hasty reading might overlook. But the natural impulse to find single meanings, and so convert symbolism into allegory, must be resisted. James's classic comment on "The Turn of the Screw" is relevant here: "Only make the reader's general vision of evil intense enough, I said to myself— and that already is a charming job—and his own experience, his own imagination, his own sympathy (with the children) and horror (of their false friends) will supply him quite sufficiently with all the particulars. Make him *think* the evil, make him think it for himself, and you are released from weak specifications."[11] Or, as Robert Penn Warren remarks, every man has shot his own special albatross. I am willing with Vernon Young to accept that Wait suggests the subconscious, the instinctual, the regressive; or, with Morton D. Zabel, to see him as the secret sharer and "man all men must finally know"; or, with Belfast more curtly, to know that Satan is abroad. This is neither evasion nor a defense of solipsism, I trust, but mere insistence that no rich work of art and no complex human experience has a single meaning. Wait is, let us say, a force; an X. But it is his role to elicit certain responses from the crew, and, through them, from the reader.

Thus our task is not to discover what Wait precisely "means" but to observe a human relationship. And the clue to any larger meanings must be found, I think, in the pattern of Wait's presences and absences. He is virtually forgotten (after that first dramatic appearance) while the men get to know each other and the voyage begins; he is something they are too busy to be concerned with. We return to him only when they have little work to do; when "the cleared decks had a reposeful aspect, resembling the autumn of the earth" and the soft breeze is "like an indulgent caress." And he is literally forgotten (by the crew as well as reader) during the worst of the storm. After he is rescued, he is again neglected for some thirty pages, and returns only with the sinister calm of a hot night and beshrouded ocean. In the two major instances, the lazy Donkin is the agent who takes us back to him, the Mephistopheles for this Satan. The menace of Wait is greatest when men have time to meditate. Thus Conrad's practical ethic of a mastermariner (seamen must be kept busy) may not be so very different from the ethic of the stoic pessimist who wrote psychological novels. The

[11] Henry James, Preface to *The Aspern Papers*.

soul left to its own devices scarcely bears examination, though examine it we must.

The pages of Wait's rescue (63–73) are central, and manage brilliantly their double allegiance to the real and to the symbolic. Here more than anywhere else, even on a quite naturalistic level, the two sides of the seamen coexist, the heroic and the loathsome. "Indignation and doubt grappled within us in a scuffle that trampled upon our finest feelings." They risk their lives unquestioningly to rescue a trapped "chum." Yet these men scrambling in the carpenter's shop, tearing at the planks of the bulkhead "with the eagerness of men trying to get at a mortal enemy," are compulsive, crazed, and full of hatred for the man they are trying to save. "A rage to fling things overboard possessed us." The entire scene is written with vividness and intensity: the hazardous progress over the half-submerged deck, the descent into the shop with its layer of nails "more inabordable than a hedgehog," the smashing of the bulkhead and tearing out of Wait, the slow return to a relative safety. Everything is as real and as substantial as that sharp adze sticking up with a shining edge from the clutter of saws, chisels, wire rods, axes, crowbars. At a first experiencing the scene may seem merely to dramatize the novel's stated psychology: these men have irrationally identified their own survival with Wait's and are therefore compelled to rescue him. Ironically, they risk their lives to save a man who has already damaged their fellowship, and who will damage it again.

But the exciting real scene seems to say more than this. And in fact it is doing an important preparatory work, in those fringes of the reader's consciousness, for Wait's burial and for the immediate responding wind which at last defines him as "symbol." On later readings (and we must never forget that every complex novel becomes a different one on later readings) the resonance of these pages is deeper, more puzzling, more sinister. We observe that the men remember the trapped Wait only when the gale is ending, and they are free at last to return to their normal desires. Thereupon they rush to extricate what has been locked away. The actual rescue is presented as a difficult childbirth: the exploratory tappings and faint response; Wait crouched behind the bulkhead and beating with his fist; the head thrust at a tiny hole, then stuck between splitting planks; the "blooming short wool" that eludes Belfast's grasp, and at last the stuffed black doll emerging, "mute as a fish" before emitting its first reproach. At least we can say, roughly, that the men have assisted at the rebirth of evil on the ship.

It may well be that Conrad intended only this (and conceivably less), or to insist again that men are accomplices in their own ruin. But the larger terms and very geography of the scene suggest rather a compulsive effort to descend beneath full consciousness to something "lower." The men let themselves fall heavily and sprawl in a corridor where all doors have become trap doors; they look down into the carpenter's shop devastated as by an earthquake. And beyond its chaos (beneath all the tools, nails, and other instruments of human reason they *must* fling overboard) lies the solid bulkhead dividing them from Wait.[12] The imagery of this solid barrier between the conscious and the unconscious may seem rather Victorian. But the Jungians too tell us that the unconscious is not easily accessible. In such terms the carpenter's shop would suggest the messy preconscious, with Wait trapped in the deeper lying unconscious.

This is plausible enough, but does not account for the curious primitive figure of Wamibo glaring above them: "all shining eyes, gleaming fangs, tumbled hair; resembling an amazed and half-witted fiend gloating over the extraordinary agitation of the damned." Wamibo could, if we wished, take his obvious place in the Freudian triad (as savage super ego)—which would convert Wait into the id and the whole area (carpenter's shop and cabin) into all that lies below full consciousness. But such literalism of reading, of psychic geography, is not very rewarding. It could as usefully be argued that Wamibo is the primitive figure who must be present and involved in any attempt to reach a figure still more primitive, as the half-savage Sam Fathers and half-savage Lion must be present at the death of Old Ben. Is it not more profitable to say, very generally, that the scene powerfully dramatizes the compulsive psychic descent of "Heart of Darkness" and "The Secret Sharer"? In any event the men emerge as from such an experience. "The return on the poop was like the return of wanderers after many years amongst people marked by the desolation of time." (As for the rescued Wait, he presents the same contradictions as the rescued Kurtz. Wait locked in his cabin and the Kurtz of unspeakable lusts and rites suggest evil as savage energy. But the rescued Wait and

[12] "Then the mariners were afraid, and cried every man unto his god, and cast forth the wares that were in the ship into the sea, to lighten it of them. But Jonah was gone down into the sides of the ship; and he lay, and was fast asleep" (Jonah 1:5). It is Jonah who must be cast out. But he has *already* had an experience of descent: "The waters compassed me about, even to the soul: the depth closed me round about, the weeds were wrapped about my head. I went down to the bottom of the mountains; the earth was about me for ever: yet hast thou brought my life from corruption, O Lord my God" (2:5, 6).

the rescued Kurtz are "hollow men," closer to the Thomist conception
of evil as vacancy.) [13]

So the night journey into self is, I think, one of the experiences this
scene is likely to evoke, even for readers who do not recognize it con-
ceptually as such. But it may evoke further and different responses. It
is so with any true rendering of any large human situation, be it outward or inward; life never means one thing. What I want to emphasize is not the scene's structuring of abstract or psychic meaning only,
but its masterful interpenetration of the realistic and symbolist modes.
Its strangeness and audacity (together with its actuality) prepare us
for the symbolic burial which is the climax of the novel.[14]

[13] One is reminded of the surrealist disorder of the cuddy on the *San Domenick,*
where Babo shaves Don Benito: the room an effective image of the unconscious,
whatever Melville intended. And, more distantly, of Isaac McCaslin's discarding of
gun, watch, compass (comparable to the tools thrown overboard) as he moves toward his archetypal confrontation of the unconscious and primitive. To the few
intentionalists who may have consented to read this far: a great intuitive novelist
is by definition capable of dramatizing the descent into the unconscious with some
"geographical" accuracy, and even without realizing precisely what he is doing. If
he is capable of dreaming powerfully he will dream what exists (the "furniture"
of the mind) as he will dream archetypal stories. The more he realizes what he is
doing in fact, the greater becomes the temptation to mechanical explanation and
rigid consistency to received theory.

[14] [Here Professor Guerard returns to "technical matters"—to questions of style
and structure, and more specifically to "the art of modulation that was one of Conrad's strengths"; in this instance, Conrad's ability to carry the reader downward
from the heroic level achieved by the crew after Wait's rescue to the everyday level
of their egoism and individuality, and upward again to Wait's symbolic death and
burial. Through a sophisticated analysis of crucial passages from these later chap-
ters, Guerard demonstrates how carefully Conrad leads the reader from the storm
test to the opposite test provided by Wait, and from one to another of the levels
of meaning identified earlier in his essay. This part of Guerard's discussion, omitted
here because of pressures of space, should be consulted by anyone interested in
Conrad's fictional rhetoric. The entire chapter is available in Marvin Mudrick, ed.,
Conrad: A Collection of Critical Essays, Twentieth Century Views series (Englewood
Cliffs, N.J.: Prentice-Hall, Inc., 1966).]

The Artist's Conscience and
The Nigger of the "Narcissus"

by Marvin Mudrick

The "task which I am trying to achieve," writes Conrad in the cele-
brated preface to *The Nigger of the "Narcissus,"* "is . . . to make you
hear, to make you feel—it is, before all, to make you see."

In this acutely visualized novel, Conrad's descriptive prose, if not
his intellect, is almost always at the tips of his senses: his power of
sensuous awareness makes luminous and substantial his account of
any external action. When he has the occasion to present an action
grand and impersonal, perhaps violent and bizarre also—accessible,
before all, to the senses—his power realizes itself in sustained passages
of description unsurpassed in English fiction.

The nucleus of the novel, and one such passage, is of course the
great episode of the storm:

> A big, foaming sea came out of the mist; it made for the ship, roaring
> wildly, and in its rush it looked as mischievous and discomposing as a
> madman with an axe. One or two, shouting, scrambled up the rigging;
> most, with a convulsive catch of the breath, held on where they stood.
> Singleton dug his knees under the wheel box, and carefully eased the
> helm to the headlong pitch of the ship, but without taking his eyes off
> the coming wave. It towered close-to and high, like a wall of green glass
> topped with snow. The ship rose to it as though she had soared on
> wings, and for a moment rested poised upon the foaming crest as if she
> had been a great sea bird. Before we could draw breath a heavy gust
> struck her, another roller took her unfairly under the weather bow, she
> gave a toppling lurch, and filled her decks. Captain Allistoun leaped up,

and fell; Archie rolled over him, screaming: "She will rise!" She gave another lurch to leeward; the lower deadeyes dipped heavily; the men's feet
flew from under them, and they hung kicking above the slanting poop.
They could see the ship putting her side in the water, and shouted all
together: "She's going!" Forward the forecastle doors flew open, and the
watch below were seen leaping out one after another, throwing their
arms up; and, falling on hands and knees, scrambled aft on all fours along
the high side of the deck, sloping more than the roof of a house. From
leeward the seas rose, pursuing them; they looked wretched in a hopeless
struggle, like vermin fleeing before a flood; they fought up the weather
ladder of the poop one after another, half naked and staring wildly; and
as soon as they got up they shot to leeward in clusters, with closed eyes,
till they brought up heavily with their ribs against the iron stanchions of
the rail; then, groaning, they rolled in a confused mass. The immense
volume of water thrown forward by the last scend of the ship had burst
the lee door of the forecastle. They could see their chests, pillows, blan-
kets, clothing, come out floating upon the sea. While they struggled back
to windward they looked in dismay. The straw beds swam high, the blan-
kets, spread out, undulated; while the chests, waterlogged and with a
heavy list, pitched heavily, like dismasted hulks, before they sank; Archie's
big coat passed with outspread arms, resembling a drowned seaman floating with his head under water. Men were slipping down while trying to
dig their fingers into the planks; others, jammed in corners, rolled enormous eyes. They all yelled unceasingly: "The masts! Cut! Cut! . . ." A
black squall howled low over the ship, that lay on her side with the
weather yardarms pointing to the clouds; while the tall masts, inclined
nearly to the horizon, seemed to be of an unmeasurable length.

Beyond this image of loosed prodigious force, the action persists with
the same sense of hallucinated clarity into an aftermath of terrible
waiting, as the men hang on, in mindless arrested postures, to the
steep deck of the ship in the quiet:

> Hours passed. They were sheltered by the heavy inclination of the ship
> from the wind that rushed in one long unbroken moan above their heads,
> but cold rain showers fell at times into the uneasy calm of their refuge.
> Under the torment of that new infliction a pair of shoulders would
> writhe a little. Teeth chattered. The sky was clearing, and bright sun-
> shine gleamed over the ship. After every burst of battering seas, vivid
> and fleeting rainbows arched over the drifting hull in the flick of sprays.

Someone, at last, can spare the energy to think of Jimmy Wait, the
Negro seaman, trapped in his cabin; and the episode accelerates to
its unexpected, appropriately grotesque climax:

> The boatswain adjured us to "bear a hand," and a rope descended.
> We made things fast to it and they went up spinning, never to be seen

by man again. A rage to fling things overboard possessed us. We worked fiercely, cutting our hands, and speaking brutally to one another. Jimmy kept up a distracting row; he screamed piercingly, without drawing breath, like a tortured woman; he banged with hands and feet. . . . We shouted to him to "shut up, for God's sake." He redoubled his cries. He must have fancied we could not hear him. Probably he heard his own clamor but faintly. We could picture him crouching on the edge of the upper berth, letting out with both fists at the wood, in the dark, and with his mouth wide open for that unceasing cry.

The whole episode is, then, an extraordinarily close and convincing observation of the outside of things. The storm, and its observable effects on the men and the ship, are heard and seen by a narrator who keeps his introspection to a respectful minimum. And this tact—this respect for appearances—contributes to another triumph of disinterested observation: the image of Wait himself.

Wait is, from his first appearance, not only an overpowering physical presence, but in the sum of external details an emblem of denial, a living judgment against the role he is, as the nigger "surrounded by all these white men," intended by prejudgment to play:

> The nigger was calm, cool, towering, superb. The men had approached and stood behind him in a body. He overtopped the tallest by half a head. He said: "I belong to the ship." He enunciated distinctly, with soft precision. The deep, rolling tones of his voice filled the deck without effort. He was naturally scornful, unaffectedly condescending, as if from his height of six foot three he had surveyed all the vastness of human folly and had made up his mind not to be too hard on it.

A moment later, we find out something else about him:

> Suddenly the nigger's eyes rolled wildly, became all whites. He put his hand to his side and coughed twice, a cough metallic, hollow, and tremendously loud; it resounded like two explosions in a vault; the dome of the sky rang to it, and the iron plates of the ship's bulwarks seemed to vibrate in unison; then he marched forward with the others.

Wait's contempt for the others and his refusal to admit, not to the others but to himself, the fact of his illness—his pride in shirking the job he is paid to do and his unfaceable fear of death—pervade and darken the entire novel. Every one of his attitudes and actions rejects compassion and the very notion of inquiry: his imperially ungracious use of Belfast and of anyone else available, his fellow-feeling with the detestable Donkin, his hair-raising animal terror while trapped during the storm and, after the rescue, his immediate infuriating recovery of lordliness; throughout, his inevitable and unacknowledgeable wasting away before the eyes of the superstitious, exasperated, reverent crew.

Only Donkin—the gutter-creature—"sees through" Wait. Incapable of superstition or reverence, a practiced malingerer himself, Donkin penetrates in a frenzy of resentment to what the nigger is getting away with: what is, for the others, obscured by Wait's heroically constructed façade of pride and mitigated by their reluctant awe in the presence of a bearer of death. There are no secrets between these two evaders of responsibility: each recognizes and adheres to the other from the beginning in the chosen role they share; and toward the end Conrad brings them together alone, hateful would-be scapegoat and pampered authentic one, in the sure-fire scene in which Donkin, murderously confronting Wait at last with the fact that he is dying, succeeds in precipitating his death:

> "I've been treated worser'sn a dorg by your blooming back-lickers. They 'as set me on, honly to turn against me. I ham the honly man 'ere. They clouted me, kicked me—an' yer laffed—yer black, rotten hincumbrance, you! . . . You will pay fur hit with yer money. Hi'm goin' ter 'ave it in a minyte; has soon has ye're dead, yer bloomin' useless fraud. That's the man I ham. An' ye're thing—a bloody thing. Yah—you corpse!"

Notably, the scene comes about only through a gross violation of the point of view: the detached seaman-narrator is dropped so that we can observe, without eavesdropping or keyholes, the two men cut off and cornered in their martyrdom; and though the violation in itself compels no distressing conclusions, it is a more important fact in *The Nigger of the "Narcissus"* than it would be in other, more loosely organized fiction. From the outset, and through more than half of the novel, Conrad has made us almost nervously sensitive to the point of view as product and evidence of the stereoscopic accuracy of the account: I, a member of the crew, restricted in my opportunities but thoughtful and observant, tell you all that I see. Such a point of view, of course, vindicates Conrad's emphasis on the outside of things and nourishes our sense of the mystery at the heart of things. When, after a number of minor violations, Conrad eventually sets aside his point of view altogether for no other reason than to present a "big scene" for which he cannot otherwise make room, we begin to distrust more than his method.

It is not so much that Conrad resorts to expedients, as that their effect is disappointing: less often to clarify, than to weaken and confuse, our impression of the minds and relationships whose inwardness they belatedly insist on. What we learn about Wait, for example, from these illicit glimpses of the "inside" makes him appear not fuller and more self-consistent, but less provokingly and hollowly mysterious, almost deflated: in an earlier scene with Donkin, his proud admission of malingering; in the death scene, his boast about an English girl friend. Wait with no background at all is far more convincing, personally and symbolically, than Wait provided with the white man's conventional notion of the black man's secret desire—

> "There is a girl," whispered Wait. . . . "Canton Street girl—. She chucked a third engineer of a Rennie boat—for me. Cooks oysters just as I like. . . . She says—she would chuck—any toff—for a colored gentleman. . . . That's me. I am kind to wimmen.". . .

Beyond midpoint in the novel, the reader is made increasingly aware of Conrad's dissatisfaction with his own chosen, and till then remarkably controlled and controlling, limitations of vision. There are the two scenes between Wait and Donkin; and the scene (perhaps successful enough to make us forget at what expense Conrad achieves it) in which the religion-intoxicated cook attempts to save Wait from perdition. From time to time, also, we are admitted briefly into the minds of the Captain, of Mr. Baker, of Mr. Creighton, and all we find beneath the gritty authoritative British exterior is a collection of soft-headed Anglophilic clichés: little cottages at the ends of lanes, smug insular serenities, and "a girl in a clear dress, smiling under a sunshade . . . stepping out of the tender sky," "the tender, the caressing blueness of an English sky." Conrad's dissatisfaction, and the expedients that issue from it in the latter part of the novel, produce nothing (with the exception of the cook's ecstatic harangue) that compares with what comes before. The inside of things, as he exposes it, looks suspiciously like sawdust.

Conrad's general reluctance to let well enough alone—his urge to explicate and adorn—extends, at moments, even into his finest descriptive passages, into the very texture of his language. Conrad may be, as some of his admirers assert, a master of metaphor, "a poet in fiction"; but occasionally, at least, his choice of metaphor seems calculated rather to impress us with his ingenuity than to illuminate his subject. A particular simile—the storm as madman—strikes him as so ingenious that he uses it twice, obtrusively, in the course of a few pages during the storm episode: "The ship tossed about, shaken furiously, like a toy in the hand of a lunatic"; "A big foaming sea came out of the mist; it made for the ship roaring wildly and in its rush it looked as mischievous and discomposing as a madman with an axe." The effect is to distract picturesquely, to diminish and make doubtful our sense of cosmic magnitude, which is being superbly established by a sequence of images not attentive to themselves but subordinated and integral to the great complex image of the storm. And when Conrad, having prepared us impressively for the first tremendous wave, describes it at length towering "close-to and high, like a wall of green glass topped with snow," the simile impels us not to see the wave freshly but only to wonder unhappily at Conrad's weakness for Christmas-card decoration in the middle of doomsday.

Still, the gravest evidence, in *The Nigger of the "Narcissus,"* of Conrad's urge to explicate, to tamper and impose, is not in the inconsistency of his point of view, or in the occasional colorful irrelevance of his metaphor, but in that aspect of his work for which he has been most enthusiastically commended: the "myth" or "philosophy," the metaphysical and moral scheme. Certainly, Conrad is aware and makes use of the natural and suggestive antitheses of life at sea, life in the image of a job to be done for nothing less than survival: authority, skill, responsibility, duty, courage *versus* anarchy, ineptness, panic, malingering, the touchy indocile solidarity of the mob. It is the effort to embody these abstractions, or rather the ease with which they are embodied, that makes the trouble. We are never free of them: they are unavoidable and commanding because the characters—it would perhaps be more accurate to call them categories of character—so fluently blend with them. What we get is a parvenu's eye view of things, a hand-me-down "aristocratic" universe in which everybody in charge deserves to be and everybody else had better jump: the "upper class," men of ability and breeding who automatically rise to power, unvaryingly steely-eyed, tight-lipped, inflexible in the face of pain and danger, like the second mate—

> Mr. Creighton, who had hurt his leg, lay amongst us with compressed lips. Some fellows belonging to his watch set about securing him better. Without a word or a glance he lifted his arms one after another to facilitate the operation, and not a muscle moved in his stern, young face.

always casually resourceful too, if a captain—

> ". . . Years ago; I was a young master then—one China voyage I had a mutiny; real mutiny, Baker. Different men tho'. I knew what they wanted: they wanted to broach cargo and get at the liquor. Very simple. . . . We knocked them about for two days, and when they had enough—gentle as lambs. Good crew. And a smart trip I made."

and everybody else the "lower class," ignorant, fickle, sentimental, cruel, easily hoodwinked, a herd to be driven, mute and stupid—

The elder seamen, bewildered and angry, growled their determination to go through with something or other; but the younger school of advanced thought exposed their and Jimmy's wrongs with confused shouts, arguing amongst themselves. They clustered round that moribund carcass, the fit emblem of their aspirations, and encouraging one another they swayed, they tramped on one spot, shouting that they would not be "put upon."

but (if genuine seamen) simple-mindedly good also—

. . . men who knew toil, privation, violence, debauchery—but knew not fear, and had no desire of spite in their hearts.

for we are reminded that there is in this preordained proletariat a subclassification, emerging from the antithesis between the wicked land (especially the city) and the innocent sea: between Donkin, out of his element at sea but swaggeringly at home in the city ("The independent offspring of the ignoble freedom of the slums full of disdain and hate for the austere servitude of the sea"), and Singleton, tireless and indispensable at sea but a tranced hulk on land (" 'What a disgusting old brute,' muttered the clerk").

Even the rather primitive unshaded oppositions proposed in these passages might serve as the philosophical scaffolding for great fiction, as at least the suggestion and initiation of character and action, especially since, in this novel, over everything impends the power and pathos of illusion, of Wait's Homeric denial. Conrad, however, is too taken with his metaphysics to go much beyond merely stating it, to aim at elaborating or examining character and incident beyond the static, repetitive point of illustration and symbol. There is no development and nothing mobile or unexpected: almost all the figures in the narrative are in fact such elementary emblems of what they are intended to demonstrate—Conrad's expressly and frequently stated "view of life"—that they would seem at once unacceptable or even on occasion ludicrous if it were not for the magnificent descriptive passages and the impressive sonorities that rescue us, periodically, from the responsibility of contemplating character. Wait himself dwindles in overexplanation, the monolithic Singleton is usually persuasive (in spite of Conrad's tedious eulogies) as a kind of Old Man of the Sea, Donkin is minor Dickens, and otherwise there are no identifiable characters at all: only men in charge (grim-jawed, nerveless, reticent), distinguished according to age, size, and rank; and a rag-tag collection of broom-pushers (credulous, rough, childlike), to each of whom Conrad assigns a monotonously recurring set of tics—the dreamy-eyed imbecile Finn; the silent, smiling, placid Scandinavians; industrious Archie; noisy, abusive, sentimental Belfast; stage machinery only, with none of the obsessive animation of caricature.

There is a kind of patience lacking, ultimately, in *The Nigger of the "Narcissus"*: the patience that presents an action, not to define it, but to let it define itself and move with a certain (however illusory) freedom; the patience that evolves characters who speak and think without serving merely to fill in more squares of the puzzle that will at length spell out whatever preestablished order the author is pleased to assert. If Conrad, eventually, enfeebles everything so promisingly imagined by his immense descriptive gift, if he must try to pass even in the climactic rite of the funeral such claptrap symbolism as the dead nigger's refusal to slide overboard ("Jimmy, be a man!" cries Belfast. "Go, Jimmy! Jimmy, go! Go!" So Jimmy goes) and the desperately needed wind that springs up the instant Wait vanishes into the sea (as Singleton had predicted: "I knowed it—he's gone, and here it comes"), it is because eventually Conrad becomes impatient with everything except the most dangerous of the novelist's privileges: the privilege (having chopped and stretched character and incident to fit his pre-established order) of philosophizing, of telling us what to think about life, death, and the rest. Inevitably, wherever the novel appears to be moving, it dwindles and ends in Conrad's philosophy and its most characteristic pose: the grandiose attitudinizing, the unctuous thrilling rhetoric, whenever the action has been cleared away, about man's work and the indifferent universe and of course the ubiquitous sea "that knew all, and would in time infallibly unveil to each the wisdom hidden in all the errors, the certitude that lurks in doubts, the realm of safety and peace beyond the frontiers of sorrow and fear":

> On men reprieved by its disdainful mercy, the immortal sea confers in its justice the full privilege of desired unrest. Through the perfect wisdom of its grace they are not permitted to meditate at ease upon the complicated and acrid savor of existence, lest they should remember and, perchance, regret the reward of a cup of inspiring bitterness, tasted so often, and so often withdrawn from before their stiffening but reluctant lips. They must without pause justify their life to the eternal pity that commands toil to be hard and unceasing, from sunrise to sunset, from sunset to sunrise: till the weary succession of nights and days tainted by the obstinate clamor of sages, demanding bliss and an empty heaven, is redeemed at last by the vast silence of pain and labor, by the dumb fear and the dumb courage of men obscure, forgetful, and enduring.

Another name for the patience that Conrad luxuriously evades is conscience: the artist's conscience, that burden and instrument about which, under whatever name, Conrad had always—as his most devoted partisans still have—so many eloquent and approbatory things to say. No scheme or pattern, no amount of impertinent hypnotic poetizing, no mastery of scenic effect will make up for it.

Conrad Criticism and
The Nigger of the "Narcissus"

by Ian Watt

So our virtues
Lie in the interpretation of the time
Coriolanus, IV, vii, 49–50

The increasing critical attention of the last decade brought forth in the centenary year of Conrad's birth a tolerably heated literary controversy: Marvin Mudrick's attack on the views of—among others—Robert W. Stallman, in his "Conrad and the Terms of Modern Criticism" (*Hudson Review*, Autumn, 1954), was answered in the Spring, 1957, issue of the *Kenyon Review* ("Fiction and Its Critics . . ."), an answer which provoked a pretty note of injured innocence from Mudrick in the subsequent issue. Their mutual acerbities may, I think, be welcomed, if only as a reminder that Billingsgate has an ancient title to not the least attractive among the foothills of Helicon; my present concern, however, is with the ultimate grounds of their disagreement and this because it involves several problems of some importance both for Conrad and for our literary criticism in general. It also happens that Mudrick amplified his case against Conrad in the March, 1957, issue of *Nineteenth-Century Fiction* with an essay on *The Nigger of the "Narcissus,"* a book which was at the same time the subject of a full-scale essay in the *Kenyon Review* by another of the writers attacked by Mudrick, Albert J. Guerard; and since *The Nigger of the "Narcissus"* has also received considerable attention in the last few years from a representative variety of modern critics, it would seem

that our discussion can conveniently be centered on the criticism of
Conrad's first masterpiece.

I

In "The Artist's Conscience and *The Nigger of the 'Narcissus'* " [1]
Mudrick grants Conrad's mastery of "sustained passages of description
unsurpassed in English fiction"; the storm, for example, and the early
presentation of Wait, are wholly successful, for there Conrad gives us
"an extraordinarily close and convincing observation of the outside of
things." But—alas!—our verbal photographer does not always "keep
his introspection to a respectful minimum"; he has the gall to tell us
"what to think about life, death, and the rest"; and there results
"gross violation of the point of view" and "unctuous thrilling rhetoric
. . . about man's work and the indifferent universe and of course the
ubiquitous sea."

The sardonic irony of that last phrase may give one pause; on an
ocean voyage the sea is rather ubiquitous—if you can't bear it *The
Nigger of the "Narcissus"* and, indeed, a good deal of Conrad, is best
left alone. True, Stallman can show how impatient Conrad was with
being considered a writer of "sea stories," but this methodological
strategy seems suspect—minimizing the importance of overt subject
matter so as to ensure for the critic that amplitude of sea-room to
which his proud craft has of late become accustomed. One may, indeed,
find Mudrick's contrary assertion in his earlier essay that the sea is
"Conrad's only element" less than final and yet salutary in emphasis;
in any case his present jaded impatience seems ominously revelatory.

Mudrick's main charges, however, are not easily dismissed. A number
of previous critics have drawn attention to the inconsistencies in the
point of view of the narration in *The Nigger of the "Narcissus,"* and
to the marked strain of somewhat portentous magniloquence in Conrad's work generally. Mudrick has only given old objections new force,
partly by his enviable gift for the memorably damaging phrase, and
partly by allotting them a much more decisive significance in his final
critical assessment. In some form, I take it, the charges are incontrovert-
ible; but a brief analysis of Conrad's practice and of its historical perspective (the book appeared in 1897) may lead both to a more lenient
judgment on the technique of *The Nigger of the "Narcissus"* and to a
clearer realization of some of the problematic implications of our current critical outlook.

[1] [See pp. 69–77 of this volume.]

Among the "gross violations of point of view" specified is that whereby the reader directly witnesses the final confrontation of Wait and Donkin, although no one else, of course, was present. Mudrick argues:

> . . . though the violation in itself compels no distressing conclusions, it is a more important fact . . . than it would be in other, more loosely organized fiction. From the outset, and through more than half of the novel, Conrad has made us almost nervously sensitive to the point of view as product and evidence of the stereoscopic accuracy of the account: I, a member of the crew, restricted in my opportunities but thoughtful and observant, tell you all that I see.

A brief historical reflection forces us to recognize that it is not really Conrad who has made us "almost nervously sensitive to the point of view," or, at least, not directly; it is a generation of critics who have developed, partly from Conrad's technique, partly from the theory and practice of Henry James, and even more from its formulation in Percy Lubbock's *The Craft of Fiction* (1921), a theory of point of view in narrative which has been tremendously influential in providing both the critic and novelist with an until-then largely unsuspected key to the technique of fiction. But there is a vast difference between welcoming a valuable refinement of formal awareness and accepting as a matter of prescription the rule that all works of fiction should be told from a single and clearly defined point of view. Yet in the last few years something like this seems to have happened, and one of Mudrick's phrases seems even to bestow on the dogma a quasi-ethical sanction: when he speaks of "illicit glimpses of the 'inside,'" doesn't that "illicit" attempt to convict Conrad of some kind of moral turpitude? To be fair we must at least admit that the charge only became criminal a generation after the fact. And, waiving the chronological defense, hasn't the time come to ask whether Dr. Johnson's point about an earlier formal prescription—the unities of time and place—isn't relevant here? "Delusion, if delusion be admitted, has no certain limitation": the reader knows that *The Nigger of the "Narcissus"* is just a story; and Conrad is surely at liberty to turn his pretended narrator into a veritable Pooh-Bah of perscrutation if it will serve his turn.

If it will serve his turn. Interestingly enough, Albert J. Guerard in his fine essay on *The Nigger of the "Narcissus"* [2] can show very convincingly that the changes in point of view serve a number of turns, and yet there are signs of a lingering embarrassment. He writes, un-

[2] [See pp. 56–68 of this volume.]

exceptionably, that, in general, "the best narrative technique is the one which, however imperfect logically, enlists the author's creative energies and fully explores his subject"; in the present case he finds "the changes in point-of-view done unobtrusively and with pleasing insouciance," and shows how they mirror the story's "general movement from isolation to solidarity to poignant separation." However, when Guerard comes to another kind of change in Conrad's method of reporting—the shift from objective reporting to lofty generalization— he comments that it is one of the "incorrigible necessities of the early Conrad," and in that "incorrigible" concedes that such variations in narrative strategy are indisputably literary offenses, although he is prepared to be good-tempered about it.

But Guerard's earlier position is surely equally applicable here; for both kinds of change in Conrad's point of view, not only those concerning the identity of the presumed narrator but also those concerning his varying tone and attitude toward what he is narrating, are closely related responses to the rather complicated imperatives of Conrad's subject as it develops. If Conrad had wholly restricted himself to the mind of one individual narrator, he would have had to expend a great deal of mechanical artifice—the kind of dexterous literary engineering later exhibited in *Chance*—in arranging for them to be plausibly visible: but this particularization of the point of view could only have been achieved at the expense of what is probably Conrad's supreme objective in *The Nigger of the "Narcissus"*; the continual and immediate presence of an individualized narrator, sleeping in a certain bunk, member of a certain watch, caught up in a particular set of past and present circumstances, could not but deflect our attention from the book's real protagonist—the ship and its crew. So protean a protagonist could be fully observed only from a shifting point of view: sometimes hovering above the deck, seeing the ship as a whole; sometimes infinitely distant, setting one brief human effort against the widest vistas of time and space, of sea and history; occasionally engaging us in a supreme act of immediate participation, as when the narrator becomes identified with one of the five "we's" who rescue Wait; and finally involving us in the pathos of separation, when the narrator becomes an "I" to pronounce the book's closing valediction to the crew as they disperse.

The terms of this valediction, indeed, seem to emphasize how well advised Conrad was not to make his narrator too immediate a person to the reader. In general, as soon as we feel that the author's reflections are issuing from an individual character we naturally expect them to be expressed in an appropriate personal vernacular; and this either sets severe limits on the range of reflection, or creates an almost insoluble stylistic problem. Both difficulties, and especially the second, obtrude in the last paragraph of *The Nigger of the "Narcissus"*; for example when Conrad writes: "Haven't we, together and upon the immortal sea, wrung out a meaning from our sinful lives?" The particularized individual cannot—in prose, at least, and since the rise of realism—be both microcosm and macrocosm without some kind of apparent inflation; such was the problem which the Irish dramatists, trying to escape from the "joyless and pallid words" of Ibsen and Zola, had to face; and in this momentary anticipation of the very note of Synge, Conrad surely reveals how inappropriate such quasi-colloquial elevation was for his purposes.

The intrusiveness of the "I" narrator, who only becomes evident in the last two paragraphs of *The Nigger of the "Narcissus,"* thus underlines the book's need for a variable narrative angle easily adjustable to different kinds of vision and comment. Until then, I think, we can find many logical contradictions in Conrad's manipulations of point of view, but not, unless our critical preconceptions are allowed to dominate our literary perceptions, any consequent failure in narrative command; and we should perhaps conclude that E. M. Forster was in the main right, when he insisted, in *Aspects of the Novel*, that "the whole intricate question . . . resolves itself . . . into the power of the writer to bounce the reader into accepting what he says."

The shifting point of view in *The Nigger of the "Narcissus,"* then, enacts the varying aspects of its subject; in a wider sense, it may be said to enact the reasons for Conrad's greatness: the fact that he was a seaman but not only a seaman, that he was able to convey, not only the immediacies of his subject, but their perspective in the whole tradition of civilization. The actual prose in which some of the loftier elements of this perspective are conveyed, however, is a good deal more grandiloquent than we can today happily stomach. As an example, we may take a well-known passage which Mudrick quotes as his clinching specimen of Conrad's "unctuous thrilling rhetoric," the opening of the fourth chapter:

> On men reprieved by its disdainful mercy, the immortal sea confers in its justice the full privilege of desired unrest. Through the perfect wisdom of its grace they are not permitted to meditate at ease upon the complicated and acrid savour of existence [, lest they should remember and, perchance, regret the reward of a cup of inspiring bitterness, tasted so often, and so often withdrawn from before their stiffening but reluctant lips]. They must without pause justify their life to the eternal pity that com-

mands toil to be hard and unceasing, from sunrise to sunset, from sunset to sunrise: till the weary succession of nights and days tainted by the obstinate clamor of sages, demanding bliss and an empty heaven, is redeemed at last by the vast silence of pain and labour, by the dumb fear and the dumb courage of men obscure, forgetful, and enduring.

Conrad himself, apparently, was uneasy about some of this, and deleted the passage in brackets when revising for the collected edition some twenty years after. He had no doubt become more aware, and more critical, of the influence of the stylistic aims of French romanticism, the only specific literary influence on his work which he admitted. The passage is, in part, an attempt to write "la belle page"—to achieve the grandiose richness of verbal and rhythmic suggestion found, for example, in Victor Hugo's *Les Travailleurs de la Mer;* and it can, therefore, if we wish, be explained away in terms of a literary indebtedness which Conrad later outgrew.

But there are other, perhaps more interesting, certainly more contemporary, issues raised by the historical perspective of the passage.

We have today an unprecedented distrust of the purple passage; the color has been banned from the literary spectrum, and "poetic prose" has become a term of abuse in the general critical vocabulary, including Mudrick's. Since T. E. Hulme, at least, we have demanded in poetry—and, *a fortiori,* in prose—tautness of rhythm, hardness of outline, exactness of diction; we have insisted that every word, every rhythmical inflection, every rhetorical device, shall contribute to the organic unity of the whole work, shall not exist for its local effect. Mudrick takes comment on the passage to be superfluous, but the grounds of his objection are, I take it, somewhat along these lines. So, indeed are mine, I suppose. At least I can hardly read the passage, or others in Conrad like it, without momentary qualms ("Should I let myself go and enjoy it? No, in real life relaxing's fine, but in literature? . . . Think of Leavis. . . ."); and yet, if we consider the Hulmean principle seriously, isn't the cost more than we are prepared to pay?

To begin with, a rather large series of literary rejections may be involved; not only Hugo and Pater and much of Flaubert but also a good deal of Proust and Joyce—not only the *Portrait* but much of *Ulysses*—Molly Bloom's reverie, for example. There are countless passages in the greatest literature which, though no doubt related by subject and theme to the rest of the narrative, are essentially set-pieces, developed largely as autonomous rhetorical units; and in a good many of them every device of sound and sense is, as in Conrad, being used mainly to induce feelings of rather vague exaltation. Nor is it only a matter of the illustriousness of the precedents; they may have valid literary justification. For, although we are no doubt right to reject de Musset's romantic certitude that our most beautiful feelings are our saddest, is there any more justification for the antiromantic prescription that our deepest or most complicated feelings—so often vague and penumbral—can and should be expressed through clear images? And why in images at all? How can we reconcile the symbolist rejection of logic and conceptualization with the fact that our minds often work by partial and groping movements toward conceptualization and logical ordering? More specifically, isn't it carrying the demand for imagistic particularity too far to assert that in literature every part of the picture must be in clear focus? Can we not, on the contrary, assert that Conrad, a preeminently pictorial writer, requires, on occasion, a chiaroscuro effect between one series of concretely detailed presentations and another? Such certainly is the way this passage—and many others of a similar kind—are disposed in *The Nigger of the "Narcissus"*: we get a relief from the immediate image, from the particularities of time and space, and this, by contrast, both brings out these particularities more clearly and at the same time reminds us that there are other less definite and yet equally real dimensions of existence.

It is probably because these less definite dimensions cannot be made real visually that Conrad's style changes abruptly and at once evokes analogies that are musical rather than pictorial. In the Preface to *The Nigger of the "Narcissus"* he wrote that one of his aims was to approach "the magic suggestiveness of music"; and though nowadays we are very suspicious of "word music," there may in this case at least be something in Coleridge's apparently outrageous assertion that "a sentence which sounds pleasing always has a meaning which is deep and good." Conrad's particular sentences here certainly suggested a meaning not lacking in depth or goodness to one of the greatest practitioners of the prose poem; for this is one of the passages by which Virginia Woolf, in "Mr. Conrad: A Conversation" (*The Captain's Death Bed*), exemplifies her assertion that in Conrad's prose "the beauty of surface has always a fibre of morality within." She goes on, "I seem to see each of the sentences . . . advancing with resolute bearing and a calm which they have won in strenuous conflict, against the forces of falsehood, sentimentality, and slovenliness"; and so brings us, at long last, away from this rather inconclusive review of some of the theoretical issues raised by the passage by forcing us to ask whether the relation of form and content in the passage is as she suggests.

To make full sense of its content we must, of course, grant Conrad the benefit of the kind of flexible and cooperative interpretation we are accustomed to give poetry, allow him his steady reliance on ironic, elliptical, and paradoxical, personification. We must accept, for example, the dependence of the paradox of "desired unrest" upon an implicit assertion by the narrator that "life," which is what men literally "desire," is in fact always "unrest"; we must also accept the personifications of the sea's "mercy" and "grace" as necessary to prepare for the final modulation of "the eternal pity," where the sea's order is equated with God's; and we must excuse the somewhat obscure quality of the irony at God's supposedly merciful attributes and at the "empty heaven" because it is evident that Conrad wants to achieve his juxtaposition of religious illusions against the only redemptive power which he acknowledges, "the vast silence of pain and labor," without undermining the traditional sort of literary theism on which the passage's elevation of tone in part depends.

The gnomic compression, the largeness of reference, the latent irony, all suggest a familiar literary analogue, the Greek chorus: and the formal qualities of the passage offer striking confirmation. The Greek chorus's lofty and impersonal assertion of the general dramatic theme depends for its distinctive effect on the impact, at a point of rest in the action, of a plurality of voices and an intensified musicality: a plurality of voices, not an individualized narrator, because the function of a chorus in general, as of Conrad's in particular, is to achieve what Yeats called "emotion of multitude," which is difficult to achieve through a wholly naturalist technique for the presentation of reality; an intensified musicality because it emphasizes the requisite impersonal urgency, as in the present case Conrad's tired and yet hieratic emphasis on repetition and balance of sound and rhythm is itself the formal expression of his controlled exaltation at the prospect of the laborious but triumphant monotony offered by the endless tradition of human effort. The placing and the assertion of the passage are equally choric in nature, for Conrad seizes a moment of rest between two contrasted phases of the crew's exertion to remind us that, contrary to their longings and to what any sentimental view of existence would lead us to hope, man's greatness, such as it is, has no reward in this life or the next, and is a product only of the unending confrontation of their environment by the successive human generations, a confrontation that is unsought and yet obligatory, although "the forces of falsehood, sentimentality, and slovenliness" seek perpetually to confuse, defer, or evade its claims.

II

Mudrick's denigration of *The Nigger of the "Narcissus"* on the grounds of Conrad's rhetorical attitudinizing and of his use of point of view follows two of the major emphases of our modern criticism of fiction; and as we shall see his operative premises are typical in much else. But we must not overlook the fact that Mudrick, who has cast himself as the spectral Mr. Jones interrupting the feast celebrating Conrad's victory over the critics, is also possessed of a marked cannibalistic trait: he cannot abide the enthusiasm of his confreres for the "modish clues of myth, metaphor, symbol, etc." In his earlier essay on Conrad, Stallman's reading of "The Secret Sharer" was his main target; but he now finds *The Nigger of the "Narcissus"* subject to the same general charge: a heavy overemphasis on "catch-all" and "claptrap" symbolism which only a naive predisposition for that sort of thing could possibly render acceptable.

That many critics have found a clue to *The Nigger of the "Narcissus"* in a unifying symbolic structure is certainly true. James E. Miller, for example, in his *"The Nigger of the 'Narcissus': A* Reexamination" *(PLMA,* December, 1951), sees "James Wait and the sea as symbols of death and life; Singleton and Donkin as symbols of opposed attitudes toward death and life";[3] the other members of the crew hesitate whether to follow the true knowledge of Singleton or the deceptions offered by Donkin; and the conflict is only concluded when they unanimously reject Donkin's offer of a drink after being paid-off—"the crew has passed from a diversity based on ignorance through a false unity based on a lie perpetrated by Donkin, to, finally, the true 'knot' of solidarity based on genuine insight into the meaning of life and death."

Miller's analysis is, of course, presented as a confessedly simplified paradigm and I have had to simplify it further; his scheme certainly has the merit of drawing our attention to a certain number of important interrelationships which we might not have noticed: but the whole conception of a neat allegorical drama surely does violence to the patent diversity of Conrad's narrative; this may be the figure in one of the carpets but what of the many other richly furnished floors? Surely no one would have seized upon this particular pattern if he had not, in the first place, felt sure that there must be some such

---

[3] [See pp. 18–24 of this volume.]

neat symbolic plot waiting to be discovered, and in the second, felt justified in giving decisive interpretative priority to a few selected details of character and incident which could be made to support it?

Essentially the same method—*reductio ad symbolum*—appears in Robert F. Haugh's "Death and Consequences: Joseph Conrad's Attitude Toward Fate" (*University of Kansas City Review*, Spring, 1952). Briefly, from the muster, in which they each challenge the order of the ship, both Donkin and Wait are seen as "emissaries of darkness and disorder, Conrad's synonyms for evil." Donkin's level is the overt, the social, while Wait's is the religious; the book as a whole dramatizes "all of the elements in the human solidarity of Conrad's world, arrayed against those forces which would destroy them," with Wait the deeper menace since he "somehow" comes to stand for the crew's "own darker natures." This analysis seems a good deal closer to our sense of the book's chief concerns, and in the main Haugh applies it convincingly; but as soon as the stress shifts from interpretative analytic summary to the attribution of specifically symbolic meanings to characters and incidents doubts begin to arise. Wait may be "a moral catalyst . . . who brings death aboard ship in many ways," but is he himself evil? And isn't it forcing the facts to say that when, after rescuing Wait, the crew return to the deck and find that "never before had the gale seemed to us more furious," this is somehow related to Wait's influence which has "undone . . . their courage," rather than to the material fact that, being on deck again, they are more exposed to the weather?

Vernon Young's "Trial by Water: Joseph Conrad's *The Nigger of the 'Narcissus'*" (*Accent*, Spring, 1952) reveals a very Galahad of the symbol.[4] If the ship plunges "on to her *port* side," a parenthetic gloss at once nautical and symbolic reminds us that this is "the left, or sinister, side"; and if Conrad compares the *Narcissus* and her tug to a white pyramid and an aquatic beetle, "the antithesis . . . is unquestionably a sidelong glance at the Egyptian figure of the pyramid, prime symbol of direction and sun-worship, and of the scarab, symbol of creative energy." It will serve us nothing to protest, for example, that this last image is patently visual, for we are in the presence of a Faith. In Young—as in many other of the more symbolically inclined critics—that faith is of the Jungian persuasion; and if I mention that I believe Jung to be a latter-day example of the same arrogant credulity which has given us astrology, the British Israelites, and the Baconian fringe, it is only because it seems to me that the kind of thinking exhibited there is exactly analogous to that in some kinds

[4] [See pp. 25–39 of this volume.]

of literary symbol hunting: everything "proves x" because "proves" and "x" are defined with such accommodating tolerance—the terms of argument do not of their nature admit either of proof or of disproof.

Most of Young's essay, I must in fairness add, is concerned with elucidating a symbolic structure of a much less sectarian tendency. In its general view it is fairly similar to that of Haugh, though somewhat more schematically presented: Wait, for example, is defined as "serv[ing] a purpose comparable to that of El Negro in Melville's *Benito Cereno:* he is the spirit of blackness, archetype of unknown forces from the depths," and the mysterious adjuration of his presence "all but deprives the crew of their will to live." Allistoun and Singleton, on the other hand, stand for the superego, and they, together with Podmore, "discover, behind the mask of a dying shirker, the infrahuman visage of the Satanic."

Wait's portentous first appearance, and the way he later becomes the chief protagonist round whom the actions and the attitudes of the crew revolve, these certainly justify our impulse to look for some hidden significance in him. Some early readers no doubt thought the same, for in the 1914 note "To My Readers in America" Conrad wrote the very explicit denial: "But in the book [Wait] is nothing; he is merely the centre of the ship's collective psychology and the pivot of the action." If we set aside this disclaimer, as Young specifically (and scornfully) does, it should surely be only for the most imperative reasons; and those offered seem to be based upon the loosest kind of metaphorical extension.

Both Vernon Young and Albert Guerard make Wait's blackness their starting point, and this leads them to parallels in *Benito Cereno* and *Heart of Darkness.* Yet it is hardly necessary to adduce Conrad's antipathy to Melville to cast doubts on the former analogy: Conrad does not, in Melville's sense, believe in any absolute or transcendental "evil," and his Negro has not done any. As for the *Heart of Darkness* parallel, it is surely suspicious that Young should apply the color metaphor literally, and thus find his analogy in the "barbarous and superb woman," while Guerard, more metaphorical, plumps for Kurtz: in any case the native woman, quite unlike Wait, is conspicuous for her heroic resolution, while there seems to be little in common between Wait and Kurtz except that they are tall, proud, have African associations, are rescued with difficulty, and die painfully. Nor is the general metaphorical implication—Guerard's statement that Wait "comes in some sense to represent our human 'blackness' "—particularly convincing. Wait, we know, was based on an actual Negro, and his color offered Conrad a whole series of valuable dramatic oppositions. These are made full use of in Wait's first appearance, where his color at once establishes his difference, his mystery, his threat: yet later in the book the color issue becomes relatively unimportant; the crew assimilates him to their group with the jocular nickname of "Snowball"; only Donkin makes a serious issue of Wait's color, calling him "a black-faced swine"; and if the narrator's own first description ends with the phrase "the tragic, the mysterious, the repulsive mask of a nigger's soul" we must remember that he is here only the spokesman of the first general and primarily visual reaction, that the color is after all "a mask," and that there is no suggestion later that the soul behind it is black.

Deferring the question of what James Wait's secret is—if any—we must surely ask why, in the absence of any convincing internal evidence or of any problem so intractable as to make recourse to extravagant hypothesis obligatory, critics capable of the perceptive felicities of Young and Guerard, to name only two, should try so hard (though not, as my present concern may inadvertently have led me to suggest, all or even most of the time) to discover some sort of occult purport in what is, on the face of it, a rich and complex but by no means equivocal narrative? More generally, why have the critics of the last decade or so put such emphasis on finding esoteric symbols? In the phrase which the hero of Kingsley Amis's *That Uncertain Feeling* uses in another connection, I can see why the critics like them, but why should they like them *so much?*

The superstition and obscurantism of our time, reflected, for example, in Young's indignation at Conrad's "fear of wholesale commitment to the irrational," will no doubt explain something, as I have already suggested; but what is perhaps more decisive is the prestige with which literary criticism is now invested. It is no longer the poet, but the critic who typically functions as the romantic seer; and a seer, of course, is someone who sees what isn't there, or at least has never been seen before. This role seems to enforce a no-doubt unconscious operative strategy along the following lines: a little like the bibliophile who is too proud to deal with anything but first editions, the critic feels his status as seer jeopardized unless he can demonstrate that he saw the book first, or at least that his reading of it is the first *real* one; his version must therefore be noticeably different from any likely previous one; and since certain kinds of symbolic interpretation, unlike the emperor's clothes, are incapable of empirical proof or disproof, they are laid under contribution as offering the easiest—and safest—means toward achieving the desired novelty of insight.

This is no doubt an unfair way of putting it; and in any case such pressures would probably have insufficient force were they not complemented by the obvious fact that the novel's length makes it impossible for the critic's analysis to approach the relative completeness which that of some short poems can attain. Given the impossibility of a full account, and the somewhat pedestrian tendency of the traditional summarizing of plot and character, the discovery of some inclusive symbolic configuration appears as the readiest way to combine the imposed brevity and the solicited originality.

In the case of Conrad, it is true, such interpretations seem to find some warrant from Conrad's own statement that "All the great creations of literature have been symbolic." The question, obviously, is "Symbolic in what sense?" and since the word "symbol" can be properly used in too many ways, it may clarify the discussion to suggest a set of rather ugly neologisms for the different kinds of literary symbolism that are involved in the present discussion.

The basic problem is to determine the kind of relationship between the literary symbol and its referent, between the narrative vehicle and its imputed larger tenor; most important, perhaps, are the distances between them and the basis on which the mutual rapport is ascribed. In the kind of symbolic interpretation I have been discussing, the distance between the literary object and the symbolic meaning ascribed to it is rather great: and so I would describe making Wait a symbol of evil, darkness or Satan, an example of *heterophoric* interpretation; that is, it carries us to *another* meaning, it takes us *beyond* any demonstrable connection between the literary object and the symbolic meaning given it.

Many examples of symbolic interpretation differ from this, however, in that not only is the distance between literary object and imputed meaning relatively great, but the rapport is established, not through taking a particular quality in the literary object very far, but through referring the literary object to some other system of knowledge which it would not normally be thought to invoke. Young's interpretation of the pyramid and the scarab would be of this kind, and since it depends upon an allusion to a specific body of mythical, religious or literary knowledge, it could be called a *mythophor*: *mythophor* would be a variety of *heterophor*, since it makes the literary object stand for something very distant from it, but the correlation would depend upon a reference to a certain story or, in the Greek sense myth; another example of this would be Guerard's drawing the parallel between Wait and the legend of Jonah.

One particular case of *mythophor* seems to require some special term because it is common and raises peculiar problems—that case in which the body of knowledge invoked is one of the depth-psychologies: this subdivision of *mythophor* could be called *cryptophor,* since it depends upon analogies which Freud and Jung agree to be hidden and unconscious; one example would be when Guerard equates the rescuing of Wait from his confinement during the storm with a "compulsive psychic descent," or when he toys briefly with the scene's "psychic geography," proposing that the Finn Wamibo figures as the "savage *superego*" to Wait's *id.*

Heterophor in general tends toward allegory. Guerard, for example, although he jests at the fashion for "analysis of 'cabalistic intent' " and cautions us against reading Conrad as an allegorical writer, insisting that the overt subject is also the real subject, nevertheless argues for a series of superimposed *heterophoric* significances which are essentially of the same allegorical kind as may justly be imputed to the Negro in Melville's *Benito Cereno.* I do not think that Conrad's work is symbolic in this way; even less is it *mythophoric* or *cryptophoric.* To make it so, indeed, is surely to emphasize novelty at the expense of truth; and the literary effect of such interpretation is to reduce what Conrad actually created to a mere illustration—something both secondary and—as Mudrick would argue—second-rate. For all kinds of *heterophoric* interpretation inevitably disregard the great bulk of the concrete details of character and incident in a literary work: just as T. S. Eliot's allegorical concern in *The Family Reunion,* for example, prevents us from inspecting the psychology and the dynamics of Harry's wife's death—did she fall or was she pushed?—so a *heterophoric* interpreter of Wait will be disinclined to scrutinize the manifest developing pattern of his character and actions. The details of these latter, indeed, will seem otiose compared to the few elements which, on *a priori* grounds, have been selected as of primary importance; and so Young can write, "Fearful of overstressing the subaqueous world of the underconsciousness, the symbol-producing level of the psyche which, in fact, was the most dependable source of his inspiration, Conrad overloaded his mundane treatment of the crew."

To demur from Guerard's statement that, on top of the various more obvious levels of narrative statement, Conrad imposed "an audacious symbolic pattern," is not to deny that *The Nigger of the "Narcissus"* is in many ways symbolic. Its symbolism, however, seems to me to be of another kind. It works, characteristically, by natural extension of the implications of the narrative content, and retains a consistent closeness to it; for this the term *homeophor* seems appropriate, suggesting as it does, "carrying *something similar*" rather than, as with *heterophor*, "carrying *something else.*" When Guerard makes the parallel of the journey of the *Narcissus* and the age-old theme of the pilgrimage, his interpretation, if allowed, and at some level of generality it surely must be, would be *homeophoric* because ships and pilgrimages, to those who know anything of them, must suggest small human communities united for the purpose of a single journey.

The terms proposed are no doubt grotesque; the distinctions on which they are based would no doubt often prove difficult to apply; and considered against the complexity of the problem and the richness of its literature, the brevity of their exposition may appear unpardonable; but if they have made more manageable the problem of what kind of symbolic writer Conrad is, and, perhaps, suggested the need for further discriminations in this general area, they will have served their turn. It only remains now to show, very briefly, how Conrad's method in *The Nigger of the "Narcissus"* is symbolic in a *homeophoric* way, working through a very accessible extension of the implications of character and event. This task, however, is complicated by the need to meet the charges against Conrad's use of symbolism made by Mudrick; for, believing that, for the novelist as well as for the critic, emphasis on symbolism tends to be at the expense of character and action which, surely rightly, he takes to be the essential components of fiction, Mudrick proceeds to argue that, in *The Nigger of the "Narcissus,"* Conrad did not "aim at elaborating or examining character and incident beyond the static, repetitive point of illustration and symbol." We must therefore attempt to show, not only that Conrad's symbolism is of a very exoteric kind, but that it does not have these damaging consequences for his presentation of character and incident.

III

Mudrick gives Conrad's early presentation of Wait two eloquent and appreciative paragraphs, but he finds the later treatment of him disappointing. It is true that the first commanding air of mystery slowly evaporates as we see Wait more closely: his curious pride, it appears, is merely the defense of an alien who is aboard only because, as he tells Baker, "I must live till I die—mustn't I?"; and his climactic confrontations with Donkin, Podmore, and Allistoun give increasingly

clear illumination to the ordinariness of his secret, his unacknowledged terror of approaching death. These later developments un-
doubtedly have a deflating effect, and if we see Wait as an emissary
from some spiritual chamber of horrors, they must seem mistaken;
but the cumulative anticlimax can also be seen as an essential part
of the book's meaning; it reveals that the influence Wait exercises on
the crew is an irrational projection of their own dangerous fears and
weaknesses; to put it in our terms, it asserts, eventually, that contrary
to possible earlier expectation, Wait is not a *heterophor*; order and
disorder on the *Narcissus* are temporary, contingent, man-made; behind the mysterious and menacing authority of a St. Kitts' Negro
there is only a common human predicament; Wait is a symbol, not
of death but of the fear of death, and therefore, more widely, of the
universal human reluctance to face those most universal agents of
anticlimax, the facts; and the facts, as always, find him out.

Mudrick, perhaps, mistook Wait for a *heterophor* and then found,
as in that case I think one must, that Conrad didn't come through;
but his disappointment has other grounds, notably that "there is no
development and nothing mobile or unexpected" in the novel. This
charge seems, specifically, to overlook or to reject the actions which
focus round Wait in the fourth chapter; for when Mudrick writes that
"Only Donkin—the gutter creature—'sees through' Wait" he is implicitly denying the picture of the case that is presented there. Donkin
is no doubt the only person who most consistently sees Wait as an
infuriatingly successful "evader of responsibility"; but everyone else
has some such suspicions, and the matter is obviously not so simple.
No malingerer is ever wholly well, even if at times he thinks so;
Wait's own agonizing divisions and contradictions about his condition
seem a psychologically convincing reaction to all the elements in his
situation; and his puzzling gratification at Donkin's insults is surely
an expression of the desperation of his wish to believe that Donkin
really has "seen through" him.

Actually, of course, only one man—Allistoun—can be said to "see
through" Wait, as we realize in the scene when, after Podmore has
told Wait that he is "as good as dead already," and Wait, supported
by the crew, has urged that he be allowed to return to duty, Allistoun
mystifies and outrages everyone by his brusque refusal—"There's
nothing the matter with you, but you chose to lie-up to please yourself—and now you shall lie-up to please me." As Allistoun explains
later to the mates, it was a momentary impulse of sympathetic insight
into Wait ". . . three parts dead and so scared" which urged him
to enact a form of Ibsen's beneficent lie by shielding him from the

deception of his own wishful illusions, and letting "him go out in his own way."

That it is the most total act of sympathy for Wait which precipitates the mutiny is surely a "development" both "mobile and unexpected," and it dramatizes one of the general themes in *The Nigger of the "Narcissus"* which is far from commonplace: pity, emotional identification with others, as an active danger to society. Nor is the treatment of the theme by any means banal; for Conrad shows that pity, though dangerous, is also a condition of human decency, by juxtaposing the Allistoun scene between two others where Wait is subjected to the cruelty of two kinds of extreme and therefore pitiless egoism: to complete the picture, we must bear in mind the qualifications implied both in the subsequent scene where Donkin brutally satisfies his malice and cupidity by tormenting Wait to his death with fiendish cruelty, and in the earlier interview where the pious Podmore, a "conceited saint unable to forget his glorious reward . . . prayerfully divests himself of his humanity" and terrifies Wait with visions of imminent hell-fire.

Symbolically, Conrad seems to be saying that although pitilessness is characteristic of the selfish, yet the increasing sensitiveness to the sufferings of others which civilization brings necessarily poses grave problems of control for the individual and for society; and by making Singleton not so much unsympathetic as unaware of Wait's suffering he may be thought to have reminded us that the older and less humanitarian order was not so easily deflected from its collective purpose. Such a reading can be advanced with considerable confidence, since, as is necessarily the case with *homeophoric* extension, it is arrived at merely by extracting a more generally applicable statement from the manifest implications of particular characters and actions; and the reading could easily be supported, both by showing how the juxtaposition of certain episodes implies such a meaning, and by pointing out various explicit comments on the softening, refining and corrupting effects of pity, comments which authorize the assumption that any events which raise such issues were designed to have representative significance.

This is not to say that Allistoun, Wait, and the rest are to be regarded primarily as symbols of these attitudes and values, and I do not think that Mudrick would regard them as "elementary emblems of what they are intended to demonstrate" unless his own criteria, both of literary character in general, and of what is desirable to demonstrate, were so contrary to Conrad's.

It is undeniable that Conrad does not give us here, nor, typically, anywhere, the kind of psychological exploration focused on the individual sensibility in the manner of James or Proust: but there is surely some middle ground between this and mere "elementary emblems." If one assumes that Conrad's main objective is the ship—its voyage and its society—it is evident that, in what is little more than a long short story, not all its complement—twenty-six individuals—can possibly be particularized; nor, on the other hand, can any two or three of them be fully treated without disturbing the emphasis, which must be on the social group rather than the individual. It is inevitable that some characters of marginal importance should be portrayed with something approaching caricature—Belfast with his hypertonic Irish sensibility, Wamibo with his inarticulate frenzies of participation; and it would obviously be very unsettling to introduce characters who were flagrantly untypical of their setting. Mudrick takes exception to the stereotyped banality of the gentlemanly Creighton's daydreams— "a girl in a clear dress, smiling under a sunshade . . . stepping out of the tender sky"; and one hastens to concede that Creighton would be a more interesting character if he spent all his time at sea counting the days until he could have another stab at Kierkegaard; but what would that do to the book?

Nowadays we can swallow everything except the obvious; and one of the reasons that Mudrick singles out this particular passage for reprobation is probably that he shares our terror of whatever may seem cliché. He finds cliché, for example, when Wait talks to Donkin about his "Canton Street girl . . . cooks oysters just as I like," commenting that "Wait provided with the white man's conventional notion of the black man's secret desires" is less convincing "personally and symbolically" than "Wait with no background" at all, as at the beginning. But the girl is mentioned in a context which gives Wait just the right kind of tawdry and hopeless pathos: off the Azores, with the crew talking of the joys of London, Wait naturally thinks of the London girl he will never see; the sick man's notorious dream of food (and rations are short) explains the oysters; while the fact that the remark is addressed to Donkin makes it Wait's last—and of course unavailing—effort to achieve some sort of triumph over the one man on the ship he has been unable to soften or impress.

Mudrick, both here and elsewhere, seems to me to have imported the cliché, and for two reasons: there is the already noted demand for a degree of individualization which is impossible and undesirable in many cases, including the present; and there is exactly the same fastidious rejection of the commonplace which, under the direction of other predispositions, causes the critics he attacks to coax esoteric symbols into the text. Both Mudrick's tendencies, of course, are closely related to his earlier demand for the sharpest possible definition in prose and in point of view: all his literary criteria, in fact, have total individualization as their basic premise.

His discussion of the moral and social dimensions of *The Nigger of the "Narcissus"* is informed with the equivalent premise, expressed as ethical and political nonconformity, and it operates with the same rude vigor. Conrad's "metaphysical and moral scheme" is based on the exaltation of the "grim-jawed, nerveless, reticent men in charge"; they inhabit "a hand-me-down 'aristocratic' universe in which everybody in charge deserves to be and everybody else had better jump"; and if we examine them, "all we find beneath the gritty authoritative British exterior is a collection of soft-headed Anglophilic clichés." We have seen that Allistoun in one crucial episode, at least, is far from nerveless, and that there are some elements in the book which are neither soft-headed nor commonplace; yet to exemplify and analyze further, or to attempt to assess how severe a disablement is involved in being an Anglophile, would probably be little to the purpose. For we are in the presence of a total incompatibility: Conrad's social and political attitudes, and Mudrick's diametrically opposed convictions.

Conrad, of course, was conservative in many ways: yet surely one can be, like Donkin, Mudrick—or myself—, "a votary of change" and still find that Conrad's picture of society commands respect. Even his presentation of the class issue, for example, has considerable objectivity: the hardships and the miserable economic rewards of the crew are not minimized, and we are given their cynical discussion of "the characteristics of a gentleman"; among the officers, Allistoun, with his "old red muffler" and his "nightshirt fluttering like a flag" is not a hero but a prisoner of the class to which his command has brought him, as we see when his smart wife arrives to collect him at the dockside; and our last picture of the ship shows the first mate, Baker, reflecting that, unlike Creighton with his "swell friends," he will never get a command. In any case, we can hardly make Conrad responsible for the fact that no ship was ever successfully sailed democratically; and we must also admit that, with all its rigidities and injustices, the *Narcissus* is a community with a genuine and in some ways egalitarian set of reciprocities: for the most part everyone on it knows and sees and wants the same things; while the class antipathy is qualified by the crew's recognition, in Allistoun or Baker, that individuals who in themselves are no way special or even particularly likeable can be wholly admirable and necessary in the performance of their roles. This dichotomy, of course, is an essential condition of

Conrad's presentation of his characters: with the significant exceptions of Donkin and Wait, their function in one sense usurps their individuality but in another it endows them with heroic stature.

All these connections and contradictions, operating within a very restricted setting, gave Conrad his opportunity for a compressed drama which could, in part, be representative of society at large. The general values which emerge are on the whole traditional, if not authoritarian; but at least they are real values, and they are really there. If George Orwell could detect in Conrad "a sort of grown-upness and political understanding which would have been almost impossible to a native English writer at that time," it is surely because, as a foreigner, Conrad could be more objective about a social order which, for all its many faults, was in some ways admirable and rewarding; while as an exile from Poland he had cause to be presciently responsive to the existence of any viable social order at all.

Mudrick's case against Conrad, then, is largely the result of the conjunction of two value systems, neither of which happens to favor *The Nigger of the "Narcissus."* On the one hand he takes to their logical conclusion a rather complete set of modern critical assumptions—the pieties of point of view, of prosy-prose, of authorial reticence about character and meaning, of extreme fastidiousness about permitted attitudes and endorsements; on the other he lets loose a teeming menagerie of personal *bêtes noires,* ranging from symbolism, the sea, and the stiff upper-lip to hierarchical authorities, parvenus, and Anglophiles. Mudrick had a very nice irony in "Conrad and the Terms of Modern Criticism" about how, in our too perceptive times, "nose to nose, critic confronts writer and, astonished, discovers himself"; one could find striking confirmation both of this thesis and of the *cryptophoric* significance of proper names by considering how vivid an image of Mudrick was reflected when he came nose to nose with Narcissus.

As for Conrad, we must conclude, I think, that Mudrick's impatient intransigence forces one to realize, both by its palpable hits and by what I have tried to chalk up as its misses, how *The Nigger of the "Narcissus"* is, in a number of ways, not at all the answer to our modern critical prayer. No amount of symbol-juggling will or should divert us from seeing that there is an important Romantic and Victorian element in his work; and, although Conrad was, of course, in many ways a precursor of the modern movement in fiction, his deepest originality and perhaps the chief unacknowledged cause of his popularity today, derives from an attitude to his society, both as subject and as audience, which has been shared by no other great writer of our century. Many things in himself, his life and his times, gave him as deep a sense of the modern alienation as any other of our great exiled and isolated writers; and yet Conrad's most vigorous energies were turned away from the ever-increasing separateness of the individual and towards discovering values and attitudes and ways of living and writing which he could respect and yet which were, or could be, widely shared. Mudrick has more than reminded us of the occasional cost in emphasis, repetition, and cliché, but no criticism has yet adequately assessed what Conrad gave in exchange. His aim—"to make you see" —has often been quoted: but there has been less emphasis on how Conrad specified that the objects in the "presented vision" should be such as to "awaken in the hearts of the beholders that feeling of unavoidable solidarity; of the solidarity in mysterious origin, in toil, in joy, in hope, in uncertain fate, which binds men to each other and all mankind to the visible world." In the centrality of his ultimate purpose Conrad is akin to Wordsworth; and if he expresses it grandiloquently, he at least does not, in the Arnoldian phrase, give us the grand word without the grand thing.

The third chapter of *The Nigger of the "Narcissus,"* for example, is not merely a magnificent evocation of a storm at sea; it is a sequence of unequaled enactments of the theme of solidarity. It begins as we experience gratitude for the efforts of the crew to save Wait, or of Podmore, incredibly, to produce coffee; and it achieves its final resonance in the famous ending when, after long forgetting him, our eyes are turned to Singleton at the wheel, and we are told, simply, that, after thirty hours, "He steered with care." It is the climactic recognition of our utter and yet often forgotten dependence, night and day, by sea and by land, on the labors of others; and by the kind of cross reference of attitudes which is Conrad's most characteristic way of achieving a symbolic dimension, this supreme image is linked with three other scenes: that where we later see how Singleton's endurance at the wheel brings him face to face with death; that where he has previously told Wait: "Well, get on with your dying, don't raise a blamed fuss with us over that job"; and that soon after where Donkin taunts Wait with slackness on the rope—"You don't kill yourself, old man!"—and Wait retorts "Would you?"

Singleton does, and the heroic quality of his labors reminds us, not only that what has been most enduring about human society has been the mere continuity of its struggle against nature, which is, as we have seen, the tenor of the ensuing paragraph about the sea which opens the next chapter, but also that Conrad's greatest art, in *Typhoon* and *The Shadow Line* as in *The Nigger of the "Narcissus,"* is often reserved for making us, in Auden's words, "Give / Our gratitude to the Invisible College of the Humble, / Who through the ages have accomplished everything essential." There is perhaps a moral for the critic here: for, in making us look up, briefly, to Singleton at the wheel, Conrad gives us a moment of vision in which, from the height of our modish attachment to ever-developing discriminations, we are compelled to affirm our endless, intricate, and not inglorious kinship with those who cannot write and who read only Bulwer-Lytton.

PART TWO

View Points

Avrom Fleishman: Conrad's Early Political Attitudes

After his initial choice of imperialist themes for his fiction, Conrad turned to the world closer to home, contemporary Europe. With the exception of a muddled short story, "The Return," he avoided the domestic problems of modern life for broader social ones. (By the time he came to write *The Secret Agent* he was able to put the two realms together in an intertwined plot.) Although his earliest work which refers to European society, *The Nigger of the "Narcissus,"* appeared almost at the start of his writing career, it was only after the turn of the century that he devoted himself to the questions that were beginning to emerge as the main ones for our time: questions about social classes, their moral values and their political vitality; questions about capitalism, revolution, and counterrevolution; questions about nationalism, war, and cooperation. This is the period in which Conrad began to write his political essays, to take a public stand on topical issues, and to write his three great political novels. It is also the time in which his thoughts on society in general, and on the societies around him, began to evolve beyond his original assumptions, the time in which he began to look back to the past in order to reevaluate his own political heritage and to formulate new attitudes toward aristocracy, bourgeoisie, and proletariat. It is these developing conceptions that inform his work in this period and give it its peculiar interest.

To measure the extent of Conrad's imaginative development, his earliest work serves as a fixed point. In *The Nigger of the "Narcissus,"* the seaman who narrates the tale expresses Conrad's ironic tone and political bias. He describes the crew with one eye on the reading public and its humanitarian sentiments, which he and the author hope to modify through a complex parable:

> Well-meaning people had tried to represent those men as whining over every mouthful of their food; as going about their work in fear of their lives. But in truth they had been . . . men enough to scorn in their

"Conrad's Early Political Attitudes" [*editor's title*]. *From* Conrad's Politics: Community and Anarchy in the Fiction of Joseph Conrad, *by Avrom Fleishman (Baltimore: Johns Hopkins Press, 1967), pp. 129–32.* © *1967 by Johns Hopkins Press. Reprinted by permission of the publisher.*

hearts the sentimental voices that bewailed the hardness of their fate. . . . Their successors are the grown-up children of a discontented earth. They are less naughty, but less innocent; less profane, but perhaps also less believing; and if they had learned how to speak they have also learned how to whine (p. 25).

This scorn of well-meaning "liberals" and of whining workers generates the plot and makes this Conrad's most didactic political tale.

In our time it is difficult to resist the temptation to read *The Nigger of the "Narcissus"* as a parable not only of class conflict but of racial attitudes. In such a reading one can see the Negro, James Wait, and the rabble-rouser, Donkin, as co-conspirators for the support of public opinion: using the same rhetorical means, they attempt to win the humanitarian sympathies of the crew. The burden of the fable would then be to check sentimentality toward the underprivileged and to affirm a conservative stoicism which accepts social evils and counsels the repression of resentments by immersion in work. Such is the implication of the description of Donkin:

They all knew him! . . . The man who can't do most things and won't do the rest. The pet of philanthropists and self-seeking landlubbers. The sympathetic and deserving creature that knows all about his rights, but knows nothing of courage, of endurance, and of the unexpressed faith, of the unspoken loyalty that knits together a ship's company. The independent offspring of the ignoble freedom of the slums full of disdain and hate for the austere servitude of the sea (pp. 10–11).

The basis of moral criticism both of mutiny and, as we shall see, of revolution is the same: they are a breach of the work ethic—not mere laziness but a rejection of the restraining values of dedication to the task, abstract duty, and subordination to authority.

Yet elements of the plot will not fit this formula, though Conrad may have intended that they should. The main parable, the Negro's evocation of sympathy from the crew, is designed to create suspicion that he is faking illness in order to receive favors and attention. But the tale takes a new turn when Wait exonerates himself by the simple expedient of dying. Since his was a legitimate complaint, after all, it is necessary to introduce new elements to sustain the tension. This is done with detriment to the credibility of the plot. As soon as Wait dies, the doldrums that have impeded the ship's passage home are ended. The implication is that the crew is right in its superstitious belief that the weather is preternaturally linked with the dying man's presence on the ship.

The characterization of Donkin, on the contrary, has no room for

8orsm. It expresses, moreover, the imposition
of the author's prejudice on the novel, rather than a discovery of moral
significance in the dramatic working of the plot. In the almost contemporary "Heart of Darkness," the attribution to Kurtz of dema-
gogic powers serves to give broad political relevance to the character
study of the arch-imperialist: "He would have been a splendid leader
of an extreme party." "What party?" asked Marlow. "Any party,"
the journalist answered (*Youth,* p. 154). The attribution of dema-
goguery to Donkin, on the other hand, expresses a political animus
that seems excessive to the "objective correlative" of the story. Donkin,
"who never did a decent day's work in his life, no doubt earns his
living by discoursing with filthy eloquence upon the right of labour
to live" (*NN,* p. 172). This net fails to catch all unionists, for Donkin
is a poor example of a labor organizer; he does not think in terms
of the working man's economic motivations. The proletarian crew
immediately shuns him as beneath their class: he is the type of what
has been called the *Lumpenproletariat,* with his hobo's rags and criminal habits. Rather than reflecting on the working class, Donkin anticipates Conrad's anarchists. He is moved by a psychological, almost
metaphysical, nihilism. When his crony, the dying Wait, asks him,
"Why are you so hot on making trouble?" Donkin fumbles for an
answer: " 'Cos it's a bloomin' shayme. We are put upon . . . bad food,
bad pay. . . . I want us to kick up a bloomin' row; a blamed 'owling
row that would make 'em remember!" (p. 112).

Just as Donkin's role as an agitator is exposed as stemming from
personal resentments, the crew—which is nominally the collective hero
of *The Nigger of the "Narcissus"*—is shown to mutiny primarily because of its personal attachment to Wait and because of childish griev-
ances aggravated by Donkin. The crew's clumsy protest against the
supercilious commands of its captain during a storm may be considered a commentary on strikes or revolutions as well as on mutinies.
The most poignant feature of the revolt is its lack of formulation.
When Captain Allistoun confronts the men and asks with a challenge,
"What do you want?" the narrator continues: "What did they want?
. . . They wanted great things. And suddenly all the simple words
they knew seemed to be lost forever in the immensity of their vague
and burning desire. They knew what they wanted, but they could not
find anything worth saying" (pp. 133–34). Conrad withholds sympathy,
not because their protest smacks of trade unionism but because their
plight is typical of the universal condition of mankind.

Even the moral sentiments of the lower classes are portrayed in an
ambiguous light; we are not quite to approve the crew's pity for

Donkin's indigence (which is strong enough to overcome their contempt for his Lumpenproletarian origins and behavior), their similar sympathy for the dying Wait, and their defense of him against Allistoun. Their ineffectiveness and cowardice in the mutiny, together with their superstitiousness and gullibility, make the novel's final judgment of their class a confused and unsatisfactory one. Throughout the tale they are presented as spineless children, and their officers compare them, to their disadvantage, with previous generations of seamen, yet at the close of the narrative they are addressed as "brothers! You were a good crowd. As good a crowd as ever . . . gave back yell for yell to a westerly gale" (p. 173).

This ambivalence toward the working class remains with Conrad throughout his career, though it detaches itself from the ultramontane politics which he had expressed in the 1885 letter to Kliszczewski. By the close of his career, as we have seen, Conrad expresses esteem for and identification with the *working* men of all classes (though he does accept the existence of a separate economic class of proletarians). But in *The Nigger of the "Narcissus"* and occasionally thereafter— as in *The Secret Agent,* where the lower-class characters, the cabmen and the charwoman, are caricatured as self-pitying and alcoholic— Conrad's sympathy with the labors and sufferings of the poor is mixed with a reserve that borders on contempt. It is an ambivalence that cannot, however, be used to characterize Conrad's politics, for it is to be found in the hearts of organicists, liberals, and conservatives alike.

Norris W. Yates: Social Comment in *The Nigger of the "Narcissus"*

The Nigger of the "Narcissus" has been interpreted as an allegory about isolation vs. solidarity, and critics have noted that one of the conflicts which disrupts the solidarity of the ship's community is that between officers and crewmen. Marvin Mudrick even accuses Conrad of a pitiless, antihumanitarian approach that presents an idealized "upper class" of officers, and a "lower" class of seamen that is ignorant, brutalized, and fickle. Ian Watt implicitly admits the charge while denying its relevance as literary criticism: "Symbolically, Conrad seems to be saying that although pitilessness is characteristic of the selfish,

"*Social Comment in* The Nigger of the 'Narcissus,'" *by Norris W. Yates. Reprinted by permission of the Modern Language Association from* PMLA, LXXIX *(March 1964), 183–85.* © *1964 by The Modern Language Association of America.*

yet the increasing sensitiveness to the sufferings of others which civilization brings necessarily poses grave problems of control for the individual and for society." [1] This note will suggest that in addition to its symbolism and allegory, Conrad's novel includes sociohistorical criticism of attempts made by reformers during the author's sea-going days to improve the working conditions of British seamen. Emphasis on this neglected theme of protest against social protest shows that Conrad saw the social tensions on shipboard as more than a purely symbolic microcosm of those on shore; for him they were a literal result of reform agitation on land.

The occasion on which the word "mutiny" is first spoken among the men includes a direct slap at the most publicized agitator for maritime reform during Conrad's years at sea. The gale and the Cape of Good Hope have been weathered, and during a leisurely interval, Donkin sarcastically compliments James Wait on his success in shamming illness. Knowles, one of the less competent seamen, remarks that they cannot all follow Wait's example: "There's six weeks' hard for refoosing dooty." He tells of how a "fatherly old gentleman," hired by "some kind people" to look for overloaded ships, talked a crew into such a refusal—"Said as how it was crool hard to be drownded in winter just for the sake of a few pounds more for the owner." The crew, says Knowles, depended upon "that 'ere Plimsoll man to see 'em through the court. They thought to have a bloomin' lark and two or three days' spree." Instead they were punished, because the ship was not overloaded—"There wasn't one overloaded ship in Penarth dock at all" (p. 390).[2]

---

[1] Marvin Mudrick, "The Artist's Conscience and *The Nigger of the 'Narcissus,'*" *NCF*, XI (March 1957), 294–95 [see pp. 69–77 of this volume]; Ian Watt, "Conrad Criticism and *The Nigger of the 'Narcissus,'*" *NCF*, XII (March 1958), 277 [see pp. 78–99 of this volume]. Cf. Christopher Morley, "*The Nigger of the 'Narcissus,'*" in *A Conrad Memorial Library* (Garden City, N.Y., 1929), pp. 28–31, and Morton Dauwen Zabel, *Craft and Character in Modern Fiction* (New York, 1957), 168–86. Morley calls this novel a "cruel" book, and Zabel refers to the crew as "closer to brutes than to civilized beings" (p. 181). See also George Garrett, "Conrad's *The Nigger of the 'Narcissus,'*" *Adelphi*, 3rd ser., XII (June 1936), 150–55, and Albert J. Guerard, *Conrad the Novelist* (Cambridge, Mass., 1958), p. 104 [see pp. 56–68 of this volume].

[2] References to *The Nigger of the "Narcissus"* are to the first edition (London, 1897) as reprinted in *The Portable Conrad*, ed. Morton Dauwen Zabel (New York, 1947), pp. 292–453. This seems to be the text most often used in college literature courses.

The original *Narcissus* sailed from Penarth, near Cardiff, to Bombay where Conrad joined her, but the roster of the crew does not suggest any concerted refusal of duty during this voyage. See Jocelyn Baines, *Joseph Conrad: A Critical Biography* (New York and London, 1960); the roster is reproduced between pp.

Samuel Plimsoll was a former coal merchant turned politician who sat as a Radical in the House of Commons from 1868 to 1880 and continued his efforts at reform thereafter. In speeches and pamphlets he charged that shipowners and shipmasters eager for more profits per voyage commonly overloaded their vessels to the danger point. His attacks won him the nickname of the "Sailors' friend," and in 1876 the first of several bills enforcing a maximum "load line" or "Plimsoll mark" on all British vessels was passed. His prominence, his aggressive piety, his habit of hurling sensational charges at prominent persons,[3] and his lack of sea-going experience doubtless induced Conrad to associate his name with one type of fanatical do-gooder who, like Donkin, brings disruption and misfortune into a ship's company.

Conrad himself sailed in the British Merchant Service from 1878 to 1894, and later professed satisfaction with the protection offered him as a crewman and officer by Parliament during his sea career.[4] In this novel, his main attack on maritime reforms was conducted through his depiction of Donkin. The cockney is explicitly identified as a universal type of incompetent and malingerer: "They all knew him. Is there a spot on earth where such a man is unknown . . ." (p. 299)? He is also a "votary of change" (p. 303), i.e., an agitator. In *A Personal Record,* Conrad implied that almost any social change was directly hostile to his basic "idea of Fidelity." He declared that "I have not been revolutionary in my writings," and added that revolutionary optimism was unscrupulous and contained "the menace of fanaticism and intolerance." Often he drew no line between revolution

---

292–93. A refusal of duty would be indicated in the dates of discharge of some of the crew and in their replacement. However, Conrad's impatience with hands who refused to sail after signing up for a voyage is reflected in "Youth" in which Marlow praises the "Liverpool hard cases" who sail the *Judea* in ignorance of the refusal of two previous crews and who work the ship until the last possible moment.

[3] David Masters, *The Plimsoll Mark* (London, 1955), pp. 122–30; G. D. H. Cole, *A Short History of the British Working-Class Movement 1789–1947* (London, 1952), rev. ed., pp. 221–22, 239–40, 243–45, 259, and E. H. Phelps Brown, *The Growth of British Industrial Relations* (London and New York, 1959), p. 72. See also Samuel Plimsoll, *Our Seamen* (London, 1873) and *Cattle Ships* (London, 1890). The former pamphlet involved the author in an action for criminal libel, and his charges against colleagues in the House of Commons caused Disraeli to ask that he be reprimanded by the House.

[4] *The Works of Joseph Conrad,* XIX (Edinburgh and London, 1925), 154, hereafter cited as *Works*. The "Merchant Shipping Act" which Conrad called "a father and mother to me" actually consisted of many separate Acts of Parliament regulating shipowners, shipmasters, and crews. These Acts were not consolidated until 1894, the year Conrad left the sea. See *Chitty's Statutes of Practical Utility,* XIII (London, 1913), 6th ed., 361–677, esp. 402–64.

and reform; the strong showing of the Liberals in the elections of
1885 meant to him that "every disreputable ragamuffin in Europe feels
that the day of universal brotherhood, despoliation and disorder is
coming apace." [5] Donkin (unlike Long, the Marxist in Eugene
O'Neill's *The Hairy Ape*) expounds no ideology beyond his vague
talk of "rights." Thus he can represent any unscrupulous self-seeker
who has a divisive effect.

One of Donkin's first divisive thrusts is his abuse of the Finn and
his generalization that these "damned furriners" should be taught
"their place" (p. 302). In this as in his other attempts at subversion,
Donkin remains essentially a landsman. In the 1880's and 1890's,
maritime trade unions played an increasing part in the agitation
for reform at sea. Plimsoll himself served as first president of the
National Amalgamated Seamen's and Firemen's Union (1887–92).
Nevertheless, in *The Nigger of the "Narcissus"* Conrad criticizes this
agitation as officious meddling by soft-hearted landlubbers. His attack thus constitutes a neglected aspect of the shore-vs.-ship contrast
that recurs in the novel—"you hear a lot on shore, don't you?" the
captain storms at the would-be mutineers (p. 416). [6] Although Donkin
has served on at least one vessel prior to joining the "Narcissus"—
an American ship from which he deserted—he remains untouched
by the lessons of the sea, and on shore at the end of the voyage he
blossoms out while the rest of the ship's company are shrinking in
stature: "He had better clothes, had an easy air, appeared more at
home than any of us" (p. 450). Moreover, in his future capacity as a
labor agitator he is specifically consigned to the earth rather than to
the sea (p. 453).

Indeed, Conrad's dislike of shore-going reformers often spills over
into direct commentary. Donkin is called "the pet of philanthropists
and self-seeking landlubbers" (p. 299), and, by contrast, Singleton is
held characteristic of a bygone race of stalwarts who had no need of
reformers or reform: "Well-meaning people had tried to represent
those men as whining over every mouthful of their food,[7] as going
about their work in fear of their lives. . . . [They were] men hard to
manage, but easy to inspire; voiceless men—but men enough to scorn

---

[5] *Works*, IX, xxi–xxii; also *Joseph Conrad: Life and Letters*, ed. G. Jean-Aubry,
I (New York, 1927), 84. In *The Rover*, Conrad associated progress, piracy, and the
French Revolution.

[6] This contrast is discussed by Thomas Moser, *Joseph Conrad: Achievement and
Decline* (Cambridge, Mass., 1957), p. 69, and Vernon Young, "Trial by Water:
Joseph Conrad's *The Nigger of the 'Narcissus,'* " *Accent*, XII (Spring 1952), 69 f.
[See pp. 25–39 of this volume.]

[7] Bad provisions for seamen were one of Plimsoll's targets (Masters, pp. 256–57).

in their hearts the sentimental voices that bewailed the hardness of their fate . . . if they [their successors] had learned how to speak they have also learned how to whine" (p. 313). Conrad minces no words in claiming that reformers with the tender-minded ethic of landsmen play into the hands of such as Donkin by luring the minds of these "big children" (p. 295) away from fidelity to what Marlow in *Lord Jim* calls the "craft of the sea." This fidelity includes involvement in the orderly routine of the ship, acknowledgment of the skipper's absolute authority, and (as Wright and Watt have observed) a mutual respect between crew and officers based on each man's knowledge of his job and "place." [8]

Other characters besides Donkin are from time to time criticized by association with the meddling of land-bound reformers. Wait is a much greater threat to solidarity than is Donkin, but part of the West Indian sailor's effectiveness arises from his softening up of the crew for trouble-makers like Donkin. Moreover, despite the collapse of the mutiny, the men continue to affirm Jimmy's wildest claims, "as though he had been a millionaire, a politician, or a reformer—and we a crowd of ambitious lubbers" (pp. 420–21). Belfast, the most sentimental of the crew, is "as tenderly gay as an old philanthropist" (p. 421) toward Jimmy. The cook too reflects Conrad's distrust of reformers. This character was doubtless inspired by some crewman on the original "Narcissus" or elsewhere whom Conrad had known, or by one or more of the street preachers whom he could have seen in London and other ports, but his surname suggests that of Frank Podmore, a co-founder in 1883–84 of the Fabian Society who, like Plimsoll, combined piety with zeal in social agitation.[9] Whether Conrad's choice of this rather unusual name was unconscious or not, he could hardly have been unaware that designations like "a conceited saint" (p. 320) and "the desire to meddle" (p. 398), and the statement that "like many benefactors of humanity, the cook took himself too seriously, and reaped the reward of irreverence" (p. 368) contained anti-Liberal

[8] "He who loves the sea loves also the ship's routine," Conrad wrote (*Works*, IX, 7; see also XIX, 190–91). On mutual respect, see Walter F. Wright, *Romance and Tragedy in Joseph Conrad* (Lincoln, Neb., 1949), p. 41 and Watt, p. 280.

[9] Edith S. Hooper, *DNB*, 2nd Supplement, III, "Frank Podmore"; Anne Fremantle, *This Little Band of Prophets*, Mentor (New York, 1960), pp. 13, 27–28, 49–50, 75. Podmore is said to have suggested the name of the society. He also wrote much on psychical research. The uncommonness of his surname is attested by its nonappearance elsewhere in the *DNB* or its supplements. True, Conrad sometimes forgot or altered the names of real persons depicted in his novels; e.g., Wait, Singleton, and Donkin do not bear the names of their prototypes on the "Narcissus." See Baines, pp. 76–77, 77 n.

barbs that readers of William Ernest Henley's conservative *New Review,* in which the novel was serialized, would appreciate.

Through the cook's behavior, Conrad suggests that the reformers' compassion is merely a sentimentality that masks an egoism more pitiless than the sternest regime at sea. Podmore brings tea and sugar to Jimmy, but has "prayerfully divested himself of the last vestige of his humanity" (p. 398) to preach irrelevantly at the dying man. In tempting a crew to risk punishment by disobeying orders, the "Plimsoll man" showed equal callousness.

Through direct statement and through character, Conrad has thus worked into his novel a social commentary on one phase of late Victorian reform agitation. His distrust of this agitation may be held responsible in part for the strength of his bias toward the officers and against certain crewmen, Donkin in particular. In addition, the social comment adds body to the over-all life-allegory. Proper attention to this social vein should discourage the tendency in critics to treat Conrad's sea tales as disconnected from their larger sociohistorical context.[10] *The Nigger of the "Narcissus"* is a tale of the land as well as of the sea.

Paul L. Wiley: The *Nigger* and Conrad's Artistic Growth

From the forest-encircled stage of the Malayan novels Conrad turned in *The Nigger of the "Narcissus"* (1897) to the larger theater of human action on the sea, and by celebrating for the first time a victory of the normal over the abnormal accomplished his most affirmative allegory. The book occupies a special place in his writing, not only for its style but also for its steady vision, its heroic tone, and a general certainty both in belief and execution which carries the narrative forward with something like the determined progress of the *Narcissus* on her path homeward to the port of London. Although its spirit is not wholly serene, the tale is sustained by a note of confidence absent

---

"*The* Nigger *and Conrad's Artistic Growth*" [*editor's title*]. *From* Conrad's Measure of Man, *by Paul L. Wiley (Madison: University of Wisconsin Press, 1954), pp. 44–50.* © *1954 by the Regents of the University of Wisconsin. Reprinted by permission of the Regents.*

[10] E.g., Moser, pp. 11–12, 134; Frederick R. Karl, *A Reader's Guide to Joseph Conrad* (London, 1960), p. 113; Leo Gurko, "Death Journey in *The Nigger of the 'Narcissus,'*" *NCF,* XV (March 1961), 301–11. Allegories of ship and crew as humanity, a prison, and a band of fallen angels respectively are stressed, to the deemphasis of more literal elements in the novel.

from the tortured self-questioning of *Lord Jim,* the nightmare vision of "Heart of Darkness," and the comic ambivalence of *Typhoon.*

Both the cosmic background and the planetary and seasonal imagery suggest a theme of exceptional scope. The sailing ship with its officers and men, voyaging alone within the circle of the horizon, is a small planet (XXIII, 29),[1] a minute world (XXIII, 31); and the curve of the journey which begins in the darkness of the Bombay roadstead and ends, for the crew, in a flood of sunlight conforms to a pattern of life fulfilled through toil. As Conrad's most complete life-allegory the book blends psychological and moral elements to such a degree that the events of the voyage may be interpreted on the one hand with reference to individual experience, on the other to the problem of human conduct within an organized society.

By taking for his actors the company of a merchant ship governed by a traditional and proved standard of conduct rather than by abstract moral principles, Conrad brought *The Nigger* into direct relation with universal human experience and thus went beyond *An Outcast,* even though the major dramatic issue in the two books is nearly identical. Both Lingard and Captain Allistoun, as well as the mates of the *Narcissus,* are rulers; and their authority is challenged by rebellion founded upon instincts capable of reducing an ordered community to chaos. But unlike Lingard, Allistoun, the one figure in the early stories who has Conrad's unconditional respect, does not stand outside society with a self-devised code of justice. He is neither adventurer nor individualist but the rightfully invested monarch of the ship (XXIII, 31); and this knowledge of his sovereignty gives him power to win in the struggle for mastery over the crew with the negro seaman Wait, a sick tyrant and emissary from the darkness. The Captain bears responsibility not for preserving a utopian scheme but for life itself against the destructive elements in nature. Since to survive the ship's company must act as a unit indifferent to personal claims, Allistoun has to prevent division that would lead to betrayal within the group. A theme of the Malayan tales thus gains new prominence and meaning; for viewed psychologically, the Captain's effort to maintain authority over the crew is a dramatic restatement of the familiar problem of mind and will. Similarly, the other officers of the *Narcissus,* unlike the men, are incorruptible not only because they respond to the demands of life but also because their will is fixed upon an object outside themselves, the task of working the ship.

Important as an anticipation of *Lord Jim* is the fact that, by placing

[1] Volume and page references are to the Kent Edition of Conrad's works (Garden City, N.Y.: Doubleday, Page and Co., 1926).

Wait among the crew, Conrad for the first time dealt with the influence of a pathological state upon men governed by a tried standard of conduct yet inclined to hold it in contempt. His statement in the Foreword to American readers that Wait is nothing more than the center of the ship's collective psychology (XXIII, ix) explains the portrayal of the negro in the dual aspect of seaman and grotesque embodiment of corrupt instinct. A creature from the darkness and stricken with disease, Wait appears on the deck of the *Narcissus* as if from the depths which claimed Almayer and Willems. Like these other hermit figures he too is a solitary harried by delusive or infernal visions (XXIII, 113, 127) and tormented in isolation by his particular demons, the cook and Donkin. As with Willems, fear is a symptom of Wait's deterioration, a death-fear which accompanies separation from the common affairs of men and so points the way to death itself. Although fear paralyzed Willems, terror consumes Wait and makes of him a frightened brute who evokes even Allistoun's momentary pity (XXIII, 118). The Captain has to contend directly against this evil which perverts the meaning of life, inhibits the will, and attracts the morbid interest of the crew:

> He was demoralising. Through him we were becoming highly humanised, tender, complex, excessively decadent: we understood the subtlety of his fear, sympathised with all his repulsions, shrinkings, evasions, delusions— as though we had been overcivilised, and rotten, and without any knowledge of the meaning of life. We had the air of being initiated in some infamous mysteries; we had the profound grimaces of conspirators, exchanged meaning glances, significant short words. We were inexpressibly vile and very much pleased with ourselves. (XXIII, 139)

Immured by his sole concern for himself and guarded by his deceit, Wait, though his influence remains noxious, offers only passive resistance to the will of the Captain. The active instrument of discontent in the crew is Donkin, and he grasps the opportunity presented by the quarrel over Wait to make his attack on Allistoun's life. In many respects Donkin appears the counterpart of Wait. Both are shirkers and egotists contemptuous of the rule of conduct essential to the preservation of the ship. Both are inhumanly grotesque, and the animal metaphors applied to Donkin transform him into a caricature of a man (XXIII, 110–11). But whereas Wait's contempt for his fellows is expressed mainly in words, Donkin's hatred seeks an outlet in violence. He desires to be even with everybody, and his weapon is the belaying pin (XXIII, 123).

From the psychological standpoint the connection between Wait and Donkin is important, for the perversity and nihilism of the former vents itself in Donkin's rage against all discipline. As will be shown later, especially in *Chance* where the allegorical situation is even more clearly defined, the relation between abnormality and violence is fully comprehended in Conrad's psychological thinking, for which reason the appearance of this concept in *The Nigger* is noteworthy. That Donkin should be the cause of Wait's death follows, moreover, since both have rejected communal law for that of the wilderness. In the cruel scene in the solitude of Wait's cabin, silent like the forest depths, the bird of prey settles upon the moribund animal (XXIII, 152).

As a foil to Wait among the men of the crew the gigantic and patriarchal Singleton is in some ways the most problematical figure in the book. Like the Captain whom he obeys with absolute fidelity, the old seaman is a pillar in the temple of the seafaring order (XXIII, 25), the personification of unhampered act as is shown in his unerring response at the moment of danger when the chain cable slips (XXIII, 26). But seemingly in order to make him a model of reliability in action, Conrad rooted out of his nature all but the rudiments of the mental and emotional forces involved in Wait's perverse behavior. In consequence he is at times only half-believable, a waxwork colossus. His lack of consciousness appears to have troubled Cunninghame Graham, who drew from Conrad in 1897 the reply that had Singleton been given the power to think he would have become much smaller and very unhappy.[2] Although this answer is in keeping with other reflections on mind as a burden in an irrational universe which Conrad had been writing to Cunninghame Graham from time to time in these years, it is also true that, from the viewpoint of Conrad's literary development, the reduction of Singleton to the embodiment of little more than unthinking act anticipates in an important way Conrad's later tendency to offset the corruption of will in hermit figures like Wait by introducing characters who survive in a world of evil through the possession of faculties almost as primitive as the "ragged claws" envisioned by Mr. Eliot's Prufrock. In "The End of the Tether," *Typhoon,* and "Falk" this device becomes the basis for irony which is not evident in Conrad's attitude to Singleton, whose strength forms a counterpole to the weakness of Donkin and Wait. Yet chiefly by virtue of his limitations he bulks almost too large in the design of *The Nigger,* possibly as evidence of Conrad's premonition that the

---

[2] Aubry, *Conrad: Life and Letters,* I, 215.

standard of conduct which had formed Singleton and the rest of his generation would come to lose meaning for a world of men of a different order. Although the officers of the *Narcissus* are the finest examples of manhood in the early Conrad, they seem to represent a passing order. In enforcing a judgment of exile upon Wait and compelling the obedience of the crew, Allistoun is really no more capable of exerting moral authority over the negro than is Lingard over Willems, although he successfully repels the forthright evil of Donkin. Singleton, who belongs so much to the past that he has lost track of change, alone remains untouched by Wait's shadow.

The death of Wait checks, however, the trembling of the balance between good and evil; and with the resolute will of Allistoun again in full command the ship passes out of the stagnant calm to complete the voyage. All of the doubt latent in the story and voiced to some extent in the Captain's scorn for the wavering morality of the crew remains for ultimate expression in *Lord Jim* (1900), in which the standard upheld by Singleton and the officers of the *Narcissus* receives its most exacting test when applied to an individual of a type foreshadowed in the crew's demoralization under the influence of Wait. The world of the *The Nigger* is still that of the sailing ship and the book its valediction. The world of *Lord Jim* is the world of steam, of the *Patna* as well as of Brierly's crack Blue Star command, an age of new men as much as of new ships.

Bernard C. Meyer, M.D.: On the Psychogenesis of the *Nigger*

Conrad's apparent neurotic suffering throughout [his] early months of marriage . . . did not prevent his creating a work which is considered a masterpiece by many critics—*The Nigger of the "Narcissus."* Begun while he was still at Ile Grande, probably in June 1896, and finished early in the following year,[1] *The Nigger* was the first of those sea stories which caused Conrad to be classified as a writer of sea tales, a designation which persists in some quarters to this day,[2] and

---

"*On the Psychogenesis of the* Nigger" [*editor's title*]. From Joseph Conrad: A Psychoanalytic Biography, *by Bernard C. Meyer, M.D. (Princeton: Princeton University Press, 1967), pp. 120–23. © 1967. Reprinted by permission of Princeton University Press.*

[1] J. Baines, *Joseph Conrad* (London, Weidenfeld and Nicolson, 1960), p. 177 n.

[2] The title of the English translation, published in 1957, of Jean-Aubry's *Vie de Conrad* is *The Sea Dreamer.*

one which continued to elicit a protest from him throughout his life.[3]
Of course the novel is a sea story, a vividly impressionistic evocation
of a ship and its men, of wind and water, of storms and near disaster.
But *The Nigger* is more than the story of a sea voyage, more too
than what its author called "an effort to present a group of men held
together by a common loyalty and a common perplexity in a struggle,
not with human enemies, but with the hostile conditions testing their
faithfulness to the conditions of their own calling." [4] More too than a
gallery of sharply etched portraits of men of the sea, the novel is a
literary tone poem whose theme is death—the grim spectacle of
gradual death unfolded before the uncertain and anxious eyes of the
ship's crew. Viewed in such terms it is clear why Conrad insisted that
the problem confronting these men was not a problem of the sea,[5]
for it was indeed one which he himself had faced as a child in wit-
nessing the slow dying of his mother and later his father. Noteworthy
is the fact that the very illness which caused their death—tuberculosis
of the lungs—is the same sickness which slowly kills James Wait, the
"nigger" of *The Narcissus.*[6] Recognizing Conrad's apparent tendency
to come to terms with painful personal experiences by actively re-
ordering them, so-to-speak, in creative fiction, there is justification for
believing that the same psychological "mechanism" was at work in
his telling the story of Jimmy's dying and its effect upon the others.[7]
Indeed, one wonders whether the very description of Jimmy's cough-
ing when he went to bed, his "wheezing regularly in his sleep" [8]
might have been based upon real models, particularly upon his father
whose final illness and death could hardly have failed to leave a vivid
and lasting imprint in the memory of his son, then in his twelfth
year. There are subtleties and nuances surrounding Jimmy's dying
which too may have originated in Conrad's own early experience.
Suggestive of a child's disbelief and inner turmoil when faced with
the bewildering image of death is the uncertainty of the crew: was

[3] Baines, *Joseph Conrad,* p. 184.

[4] "Stephen Crane" in *Last Essays,* p. 94.

[5] G. Jean-Aubry, *Joseph Conrad, Life and Letters* (Garden City, Doubleday &
Company, Inc., 1927), II, p. 342. Letter to Henry Canby, April 7, 1924.

[6] And presumably also Yanko Gooral of "Amy Foster."

[7] Suggestive of this attempt to master an early trauma through active repetition
is the message sent to Garnett by Conrad as he was finishing the novel: "Nigger
died on the 7th at 6 P.M." To which he added, "I can't eat—I dream—nightmares—
and scare my wife." In the context of the present hypothesis it is regrettable that
Conrad failed to mention the content of those dreams. E. Garnett, ed., *Letters from
Conrad,* 1895–1924 (Indianapolis, Bobbs-Merrill, 1928), p. 83. Letter of Jan. 10, 1897.

[8] *The Nigger of the "Narcissus,"* p. 24.

Jimmy really sick, or was he faking and exploiting them? They despise him, yet they cannot refrain from mothering him tenderly and from rescuing him when he becomes entombed in his cabin during the storm.[9] "We hated James Wait. We could not get rid of the monstrous suspicion that this astounding black man was shamming sick, had been malingering heartlessly in the face of our toil, of our scorn, of our patience—and now he was malingering in the face of our devotion —in the face of death." [10]

Jimmy is not the only demoralizing force on board the *Narcissus*. The solidarity of the crew and its devotion to duty is also threatened by the troublemaker Donkin, who seeks to incite the others to mutiny. Indeed it is Karl's view that these two men are the first of a long line of Conradian anarchists; "not men who throw bombs, but those who refuse their duties and know nothing of courage and endurance and loyalty; men who know only of their rights." [11] But if the Negro James Wait is to be viewed as an "anarchist" he may also be regarded as a particularly sharply delineated example of the "outsider," the disruptive alien, who elicits hatred and distrust, and occasionally compassion from the crowd, as well as from the reader. He would appear again in Conrad's fiction, notably as the Central European castaway, Yanko Gooral, washed up on the English coast, and as the Jew, Señor Hirsch of *Nostromo*. In a larger sense, however, the designation "outsider" is applicable to virtually every major character in Conrad's fiction, and in the course of the present study evidence will be offered which suggests that aside from whatever real models he may have used in fashioning these individuals alienated from their surroundings, ultimately they represent multiple self-portraits of the author himself. Viewed in this light the picture of James Wait as a childlike helpless creature, whose physical sickness appears to be admixed with malingering, and who still succeeds in holding those about him in a kind of "weird servitude," [12] may be regarded as an incisive and scornful confession. Support for this hypothesis is not wanting, for there is abundant evidence that these same attributes were always present in Conrad's personality, and conspicuously so after his marriage.

That during the early troubled months of married life he was able to compose a generally acknowledged masterpiece is noteworthy, for his other literary efforts of that time were somewhat less than that.

[9] The claustrophobia implicit in this scene will be discussed in a later chapter.
[10] *The Nigger of the "Narcissus,"* pp. 72–73.
[11] F. Karl, *A Reader's Guide to Joseph Conrad* (New York, Noonday, 1960), p. 112.
[12] *The Nigger of the "Narcissus,"* p. 43.

. . . If "An Outpost" stands above the rest of the short stories written during this period it should be noted that it is the only story of this era—except *The Nigger*—which is virtually devoid of women and love interest. Indeed, it would seem likely that it was this same remoteness from any overt allusion to the emotional conflicts which Conrad's courtship and marriage had apparently intensified, that made *The Nigger* "possible." In this story with "its conditions of complete isolation from all land entanglements," [13] Conrad could escape from the stifling atmosphere of a close relationship, and, of probably even greater importance, from the oppressive embrace of physical intimacy. It is true he wrote of death (did he long for it?), but he wrote easily and produced a work that may be said to fulfill his definition of artistic aim: ". . . to aspire to the plasticity of sculpture, to the colour of painting, and to the magic suggestiveness of music—which is the art of arts." [14] Unhindered by the burdens of love and sexuality that had caused his other literary craft to drag or founder in their course, the *Narcissus* moved swiftly, a thing of grace and beauty, carrying her creator, in his fancy, once again into the familiar serenity of the open seas.

[13] Jean-Aubry, *Life and Letters*, II, p. 342. Letter to Henry Canby, April 7, 1924.
[14] *The Nigger of the "Narcissus,"* p. xiii.

Chronology of Important Dates

	Conrad	The Age
1853		Beginning of Crimean War; renewed revolutionary activity in Poland.
1857	December 3, Conrad born near Berdichev in the Ukraine, only child of writer-revolutionary Apollo Nałęcz Korzeniowski and wife Evelina.	
1862	Family exiled from Poland to northern Russia.	
1865, 1869	Mother (age 32), then father (age 49) die of tuberculosis.	
1873		Carlist warfare resumes in Spain.
1874	Joins French merchant navy, first voyage December.	
1876		Founding of International Association for Exploration and Civilization in Africa, King Leopold of Belgium president.
1878	Attempts suicide after involvement in Carlist gun-running, love affair, gambling. Enters British merchant marine.	
1881		First merchant vessel built entirely of steel, capable of crossing Atlantic in a week.

1884	Voyage of *Narcissus,* April 28 to October 17, Conrad second mate.	
1886	Receives Master's certificate.	
1890	Goes to Congo as captain of river steamer.	
1894		Greenwich Bomb Outrage (anarchist attempt to bomb Greenwich Observatory).
1895	Publishes first novel, *Almayer's Folly.* Sea years end.	
1896	Married to Jessie George.	
1899		South African War (Boer War) begins.
1899–1915	Period of major literary activity and increasing concern with social problems. "Heart of Darkness" 1899; *Lord Jim* 1900; *Nostromo* 1904; *The Secret Agent* 1907; "The Secret Sharer" 1910; *Under Western Eyes* 1911; *Victory* 1915.	
1914	Revisits Poland.	World War I begins.
1917		Bolshevik revolution in Russia.
1918		Armistice.
1923	*The Rover,* last completed novel. Visits United States.	
1924	Dies August 3. Buried at Canterbury.	

Notes on the Editor and Contributors

JOHN A. PALMER, Professor of English and Dean of the School of Letters and Science at California State College, Los Angeles, is the author of *Joseph Conrad's Fiction: A Study in Literary Growth.*

AVROM FLEISHMAN, Associate Professor of English at Johns Hopkins University, is the author of *Conrad's Politics: Community and Anarchy in the Fiction of Joseph Conrad* and *A Reading of Mansfield Park.*

ALBERT J. GUERARD, Professor of English at Stanford University, is a practicing novelist and author of critical books on Bridges, Hardy, Gide, and Conrad. He is editor of the *Twentieth Century Views* volume, *Hardy: A Collection of Critical Essays.*

BERNARD C. MEYER, M.D., is Clinical Professor of Psychiatry at the Mt. Sinai School of Medicine, and is the author of *Joseph Conrad: A Psychoanalytic Biography,* as well as numerous technical articles.

JAMES E. MILLER, JR., Professor of English at the University of Chicago, is author and editor of numerous anthologies and critical studies, including works on Fitzgerald, Melville, and Whitman.

MARVIN MUDRICK, Professor of English and Provost of the College of Creative Studies at the University of California, Santa Barbara, is the author of *Jane Austen: Irony as Defense and Discovery.* He is editor of the Twentieth Century Views volume, *Conrad: A Collection of Critical Essays.*

CECIL SCRIMGEOUR, Educational Officer for the Workers' Educational Association, has taught in the University of Keele and the University of Oxford Delegacy for Extra-mural Studies. Among his publications are essays in *Critical Quarterly* and *Essays in Criticism.*

IAN WATT, Professor of English and Chairman of the Department at Stanford University, is the author of *The Rise of the Novel: Studies in Defoe, Richardson, and Fielding,* and of numerous critical articles and editions. He is editor of the Twentieth Century Views volume, *Jane Austen: A Collection of Critical Essays.*

PAUL L. WILEY, Professor of English at the University of Wisconsin, is a literary historian and the author of *Conrad's Measure of Man* and *Novelist of Three Worlds: Ford Madox Ford.*

NORRIS W. YATES, Professor of English at Iowa State University, is the author of critical works on Günter Grass and on American humorists of the twentieth century. His most recent book is the Twayne *Robert Benchley.*

VERNON YOUNG, Film Editor of *The Hudson Review,* is a cinema and literary critic now resident in Europe. Among his publications are essays in *Kenyon Review, The Nation, Film Quarterly,* and *Dialogue.* He is currently finishing a book on the cultural context of Ingmar Bergman's films.

Selected Bibliography

Editions

The standard edition is *The Works of Joseph Conrad* (London and Toronto: J. M. Dent & Sons, Ltd., 1923–28). Most other Dent and Doubleday editions have identical pagination. Morton Dauwen Zabel, ed., *The Portable Conrad* (New York: The Viking Press, Inc., 1947) reprints the first edition of *The Nigger of the "Narcissus."*

Secondary Sources

The selections represented in this volume comprise the most significant critical commentary specifically on *The Nigger of the "Narcissus."* Beyond these selections, the reader will profit most from more general studies of Conrad which may in turn throw further light on the *Nigger*. Guerard's and Meyer's books are basic reading for students of Conrad. Both writers have helped establish the currently fashionable view of Conrad's career as a case of "achievement and decline," in which the *Nigger*, a major early work, is held to be superior to his later fiction and to other early works in which his creative energies seem to have been impeded. A more recent study, John A. Palmer's *Joseph Conrad's Fiction: A Study in Literary Growth* (Ithaca: Cornell University Press, 1968) proposes major revisions in the "achievement and decline" theory, dividing Conrad's fiction instead into three major periods of growth, and viewing the *Nigger* in part as a preparation for Conrad's early Marlow tales. Ian Watt's "Joseph Conrad: Alienation and Commitment," in H. S. Davies and G. Watson, eds., *The English Mind* (Cambridge: At the University Press, 1964), pp. 257–78, examines Conrad's commitment to "solidarity" as a counterbalance to the alienation of the modern mind, and identifies forces in the history of ideas and in Conrad's own background which help account for his ethical stance. J. Hillis Miller's *Poets of Reality: Six Twentieth-Century Writers* (Cambridge, Mass.: Belknap Press, 1965), pp. 13–67, examines Conrad's place as an exponent of modern perspectivism and nihilism, and their effects on metaphor and conceptual language in his work, thus touching upon important issues raised by the

Nigger and its Preface. Among older critical studies, the following are still valuable: Joseph Warren Beach, *The Twentieth Century Novel: Studies in Technique* (New York: Appleton-Century, 1932), pp. 337–65, for its treatment of "impressionism" and of the problem of point of view in the *Nigger;* John D. Gordan, *Joseph Conrad: The Making of a Novelist* (Cambridge: Harvard University Press, 1940), for its identification of significant manuscript changes and its summary of early reactions to Conrad's work; and Morton Dauwen Zabel, *Craft and Character in Modern Fiction* (New York: The Viking Press, Inc., 1957), pp. 147–227, for its keen historical sense and clear awareness of the thematic relations between the *Nigger* and Conrad's other works. Conrad's sea experience has received considerable attention from biographers and scholars: Jerry Allen, *The Sea Years of Joseph Conrad* (Garden City, N.Y.: Doubleday & Company, Inc., 1965); Gerard Jean-Aubry, *The Sea Dreamer: A Definitive Biography of Joseph Conrad* (Garden City, N.Y.: Doubleday & Company, Inc., 1957); Jocelyn Baines, *Joseph Conrad: A Critical Biography* (New York: McGraw-Hill Book Company, 1960); and Norman Sherry, *Conrad's Eastern World* (Cambridge: At the University Press, 1966). Baines is the standard biography. Along with Conrad's own letters and essays (notably *The Mirror of the Sea* and *A Personal Record*), these works help to delineate the experiences and attitudes that were to be given artistic form in *The Nigger of the "Narcissus."*

TWENTIETH CENTURY
INTERPRETATIONS

MAYNARD MACK, *Series Editor*
Yale University

NOW AVAILABLE
Collections of Critical Essays
ON

ADVENTURES OF HUCKLEBERRY FINN
ALL FOR LOVE
THE AMBASSADORS
ARROWSMITH
AS YOU LIKE IT
BLEAK HOUSE
THE BOOK OF JOB
THE CASTLE
DOCTOR FAUSTUS
DON JUAN
DUBLINERS
THE DUCHESS OF MALFI
ENDGAME
EURIPIDES' ALCESTIS
THE FALL OF THE HOUSE OF USHER
THE FROGS
GRAY'S ELEGY
THE GREAT GATSBY
GULLIVER'S TRAVELS
HAMLET
HARD TIMES
HENRY IV, PART TWO

(continued on next page)

(continued from previous page)

HENRY V
THE ICEMAN COMETH
JULIUS CAESAR
KEATS'S ODES
LIGHT IN AUGUST
LORD JIM
MUCH ADO ABOUT NOTHING
THE NIGGER OF THE "NARCISSUS"
OEDIPUS REX
THE OLD MAN AND THE SEA
PAMELA
THE PLAYBOY OF THE WESTERN WORLD
THE PORTRAIT OF A LADY
A PORTRAIT OF THE ARTIST AS A YOUNG MAN
THE PRAISE OF FOLLY
PRIDE AND PREJUDICE
THE RAPE OF THE LOCK
THE RIME OF THE ANCIENT MARINER
ROBINSON CRUSOE
SAMSON AGONISTES
THE SCARLET LETTER
SIR GAWAIN AND THE GREEN KNIGHT
SONGS OF INNOCENCE AND OF EXPERIENCE
THE SOUND AND THE FURY
THE TEMPEST
TESS OF THE D'URBERVILLES
TOM JONES
TWELFTH NIGHT
UTOPIA
WALDEN
THE WASTE LAND
WOMEN IN LOVE
WUTHERING HEIGHTS